PROBLEM SOLVING AND PROGRAM DESIGN IN C

Custom Supplement for Ryerson University

Taken from:

Problem Solving and Program Design in C, Fifth Edition
by Jeri R. Hanly and Elliot B. Koffman

C Program Design for Engineers, Second Edition
by Jeri R. Hanly and Elliot B. Koffman

Taken from:

Problem Solving and Program Design in C, Fifth Edition
by Jeri R. Hanly and Elliot B. Koffman
Copyright © 2007 by Pearson Education, Inc.
Published by Addison Wesley
Boston, Massachusetts 02116

C Program Design for Engineers, Second Edition
by Jeri R. Hanly and Elliot B. Koffman
Copyright © 2001 by Addison Wesley Longman, Inc.
A Pearson Education Company
Boston, Massachusetts 02116

This special edition published in cooperation with Pearson Custom Publishing.

All trademarks, service marks, registered trademarks, and registered service marks are the property
of their respective owners and are used herein for identification purposes only.

Printed in Canada

10 9 8 7 6 5 4 3 2 1

ISBN 0-536-53212-5

2007200405

ED

Please visit our web site at *www.pearsoncustom.com*

PEARSON CUSTOM PUBLISHING
501 Boylston Street, Suite 900, Boston, MA 02116
A Pearson Education Company

CONTENTS

The following content was taken from *C Program Design for Engineers*, Second Edition by Jeri R. Hanly and Elliot B. Koffman

The following content was taken from *Problem Solving and Program Design in C*, Fifth Edition by Jeri R. Hanly and Elliot B. Koffman

C Program Design for Engineers, Second Edition
by Jeri R. Hanly and Elliot B. Koffman

CHAPTER 2

Overview of C

QUICK-CHECK EXERCISES

1. What value is assigned to the type double variable x by the statement

   ```
   x = 25.0 * 3.0 / 2.5;
   ```

2. What value is assigned to x by the following statement, assuming x is 10.0?

   ```
   x = x - 20.0;
   ```

3. Show the exact form of the output line displayed when x is 3.456.

   ```
   printf("Three values of x are %4.1f*%5.2f*%.3f\n",
           x, x, x);
   ```

4. Show the exact form of the output line when n is 345.

   ```
   printf("Three values of n are %4d*%5d*%d\n", n, n, n);
   ```

5. What data types would you use to represent the following items: number of experiments run in a month, a letter grade on an exam, the severity of an earthquake on the Richter scale?

6. In which step of the software development method are the problem inputs and outputs identified?

7. If function scanf is getting two numbers from the same line of input, what characters should be used to separate them?

8. How does the computer determine how many data values to get from the input device when a scanf operation is performed?

9. In an interactive program, how does the program user know how many data values to enter when the scanf function is called?
10. Does the compiler detect syntax or run-time errors?

ANSWERS TO QUICK-CHECK EXERCISES

1. `30.0`
2. `-10.0`
3. `Three values of x are ■3.5*■3.46*3.456` (■ = 1 blank)
4. `Three values of n are ■345*■■345*345`
5. `int, char, double`
6. analysis
7. blanks
8. It depends on the number of placeholders in the format string.
9. from reading the prompt
10. syntax errors

REVIEW QUESTIONS

1. What type of information should be specified in the block comment at the very beginning of the program?
2. Which variables below are syntactically correct?

    ```
    income        two fold
    1time         c3po
    int           income#1
    Tom's         item
    ```

3. What is illegal about the following program fragment?

    ```
    #include <stdio.h>
    #define PI 3.14159

    int
    main(void)
    {
         double c, r;

         scanf("%lf%lf", c, r);
         PI = c / (2 * r);
         . . .
    }
    ```

4. Stylistically, which of the following identifiers would be good choices for names of constant macros?

```
gravity    G    MAX_SPEED    Sphere_Size
```

5. Write the data requirements, necessary formulas, and algorithm for Programming Project 6 in the next section.
6. The average pH of citrus fruits is 2.2, and this value has been stored in the variable avg_citrus_pH. Provide a statement to display this information in a readable way.
7. List three standard data types of C.
8. Convert the program statements below to take input data and echo it in batch mode.

```
printf("Enter two characters> ");
scanf("%c%c", &c1, &c2);
printf("Enter three integers separated by spaces> ");
scanf("%d%d%d", &n, &m, &p);
```

9. Write a program fragment that allows for the input of an integer value, doubles it, subtracts 10, and displays the result.

PROGRAMMING PROJECTS

1. Write a program to convert a volume in milliliters to fluid ounces.

Data Requirements

Problem Input
```
int ml        /* volume in milliliters  */
```

Problem Output
```
double fl_oz /* volume in fluid ounces */
```

Relevant Formula
fluid_ounces = 0.034 (*milliliters*)

2. Write a program to take a depth (in kilometers) inside the Earth as input data; compute and print the temperature at this depth in degrees Celsius and degrees Fahrenheit.

Data Requirements

Problem Input
```
double depth              /* depth in km */
```

Problem Outputs
```
double celsius            /* temperature in degrees
                             Celsius    */
double fahr               /* temperature in degrees
                             Fahrenheit */
```

Relevant Formulas

$celsius = 10 \; (depth) + 20$ `/* Celsius temperature at`
                                      `depth in km */`

$fahrenheit = 1.8 \; (celsius) + 32$

3. Write a program that predicts the score needed on a final exam to achieve a desired grade in a course. The program should interact with the user as follows:

```
Enter desired grade> B
Enter minimum average required> 79.5
Enter current average in course> 74.6
Enter how much the final counts
as a percentage of the course grade> 25

You need a score of 94.20 on the final to get a B.
```

In the example shown, the final counts 25 percent of the course grade.

4. Write a program that calculates how many Btus of heat are delivered to a house given the number of gallons of oil burned and the efficiency of the house's oil furnace. Assume that a barrel of oil (42 gallons) has an energy equivalent of 5,800,000 Btu. (*Note:* This number is too large to represent as an `int` on most personal computers.) For one test use an efficiency of 65 percent and 100 gallons of oil.

5. If a human heart beats on the average of once a second, how many times does the heart beat in a lifetime of 78 years? (Use 365.25 for days in a year.) Rerun your program for a heart rate of 75 beats per minute.

6. Write a program that takes the length and width of a rectangular yard and the length and width of a rectangular house situated in the yard. Your program should calculate and display the time required to cut the grass at the rate of two square feet a second.

7. Metro City Planners proposes that a community develop a new water supply by replacing all the community's toilets with low-flush models that use only 2 liters per flush. Assume that there is about 1 toilet for every 3 persons, that existing toilets use an average of 15 liters per flush, that a toilet is flushed on average 14 times per day, and that the cost to install each new toilet is $150. Write a program that would estimate the magnitude of the water saved (liters/day) and the cost of this new water supply based on the community's population.

8. Write a program that calculates how far a satellite travels in one rotation about the earth, given the satellite's altitude in kilometers. Use 12,730 km as the Earth's diameter.

CHAPTER 3

Data Types, Operators,
and
Simple Functions

QUICK-CHECK EXERCISES

1. If a is 4, b is 3.8, and c is 2, what is the value of this expression?

   ```
   (int)b + a * c
   ```

2. How would you write this expression in C? Assume all variables are of type `double` and are named with single letters.

$$\frac{\sqrt{a} + 5}{cd - |e|}$$

3. Assume that n and d represent positive integers. Write a more concise expression that is equivalent to

   ```
   n - n / d * d
   ```

4. How is a function executed in a program?
5. What is the purpose of a function's input arguments?
6. Write this equation as a C statement:

$$y = (e^{a \ln b})^2$$

7. What does the following function do?

```
void
nonsense(void)
{
        printf("*****\n");
        printf("*   *\n");
        printf("*****\n");
}
```

8. What does the following main function do?

```
int
main(void)
{
        nonsense();
        nonsense();
        nonsense();
        return (0);
}
```

ANSWERS TO QUICK-CHECK EXERCISES

1. 11
2. `(sqrt(a) + 5) / (c * d - fabs(e))`
3. `n % d`
4. It is called into execution by a function call, that is, the function name followed by its arguments in parentheses.
5. A function's input arguments take information into a function.
6. `y = pow(exp(a * log(b)),2);`
7. It displays a rectangle of asterisks.
8. It displays three rectangles of asterisks on top of one another.

REVIEW QUESTIONS

1. An explicit conversion from one data type to another is called a(n) _____.
2. What are three advantages of using functions?
3. When is a function executed, and where should a user-defined function appear in the program source file?
4. Write a program that prompts the user for the lengths of two legs of a right triangle and makes use of the pow and sqrt functions to compute the length of the hypotenuse using the Pythagorean theorem. Include a function that gives instructions to the user.

5. Write a program that draws a rectangle made of a double border of asterisks. Use two functions: `draw_sides` and `draw_line`.
6. What are the advantages of data type `int` over data type `double`? What are the advantages of type `double` over type `int`?
7. List and explain three computational errors that may occur in type `double` expressions.

PROGRAMMING PROJECTS

1. Write a program that calculates the distance in kilometers between two locations on the Earth. The program should first call a user-defined function that displays a description of its purpose. Then it should prompt the user to enter the latitude and longitude of each location as a signed angle in degrees and minutes. The distance between the two locations (s) can be calculated as

$$s = 2 \times r \times \sin^{-1}\sqrt{\sin^2\left(\frac{\phi_0 - \phi_1}{2}\right) + \cos \phi_1 \cos \phi_0 \sin^2\left(\frac{\lambda_0 - \lambda_1}{2}\right)}$$

where r is the Earth's radius (approximately 6365 km); (ϕ_0, λ_0) represents the latitude and longitude of one location; and (ϕ_1, λ_1) is the other location. The formula assumes that latitudes and longitudes are in radians, with north latitudes and east longitudes being positive and south latitudes and west longitudes being negative. Notice that you will need to convert the latitudes and longitudes to radian values to use the formula shown. For one test, calculate the distance between longitude 84° 30' W, latitude 10° 30'N (Costa Rica) and longitude 71° 5' W, latitude 42° 24' N (Boston).

2. Write a computer program that computes the duration of a projectile's flight and its height above ground when it reaches the target. As part of your solution, write and call a function that displays instructions to the program user.

Problem Constant
```
G 32.17 /* gravitational constant                              */
```

Problem Inputs
```
double theta /* input - angle (radians) of elevation   */
double distance /* input - distance (ft) to target      */
double velocity /* input - projectile velocity
                          (ft/sec)                        */
```

Problem Outputs
```
double time   /* output - time (sec) of flight           */
double height /* output - height at impact               */
```

[1]John P. Snyder, "Map Projections—A Working Manual," *U.S. Geological Survey Professional Paper 1395*, 1987.

Relevant Formulas

$$time = \frac{distance}{velocity \times cos\,(theta)}$$

$$height = velocity \times sin(theta) \times time - \frac{g \times time^2}{2}$$

Try your program on these data sets.

Inputs	Data Set 1	Data Set 2
Angle of elevation	0.3 radian	0.71 radian
Velocity	800 ft/sec	1,600 ft/sec
Distance to target	11,000 ft	78,670 ft

3. Write a program that computes the speed of sound (a) in air of a given temperature T (°F). Use the formula

$$a = 1086 \text{ ft/s} \sqrt{\frac{5T + 2297}{2457}}$$

Caution: Be sure your program does not lose the fractional part of the quotient in the formula shown. Write and call a function that displays instructions to the user.

4. Write a program that takes a positive number with a fractional part and rounds it to two decimal places. For example, 32.4851 would round to 32.49, and 32.4431 would round to 32.44. (Hint: See Problem 2b in the Self-Check Exercises for Section 3.4.)

5. Write a program that estimates the temperature in a freezer (in °C) given the elapsed time (hours) since a power failure. Assume that this temperature (T) is given by

$$T = \frac{4t^2}{t + 2} - 20$$

where t is the time since the power failure. Your program should call a user-defined function that displays a description of the program's purpose and should then prompt the user to enter how long it has been since the start of the power failure in whole hours and minutes. Note that you will need to convert the elapsed time into hours. For example, if the user entered 2 30 (2 hours 30 minutes), you would need to convert this to 2.5 hours.

6. A cyclist coasting on a level road slows from a speed of 10 mi/hr to 2.5 mi/hr in one minute. Write a computer program that calculates the cyclist's constant rate of acceleration and determines how long the cyclist will take to come to rest, given an initial speed of 10 mi/hr. (Hint: Use the equation

$$a = \frac{v_f - v_i}{t}$$

where a is acceleration, t is time interval, v_i is initial velocity, and v_f is the final velocity.) Write and call a function that displays instructions to the program user.

7. An electron moving freely in a magnetic field emits electromagnetic radiation. Physicists and engineers can measure this radiation and can then infer information about the electron. From physics, we know that

$$frequency = \frac{speed\ of\ light}{wavelength}$$

where the speed of light is 3.0E8 meters/second. It is also true that

$$energy = h \times frequency$$

where h is Planck's constant, equal to 6.63E-34 joule-seconds. Write a program that takes wavelength observed in meters as input and displays the frequency of the radiation generated by the electron, in hertz, and the energy of a photon emitted by the electron, in joules. Use variables of type double for all data, and try out your program for wavelengths in the range 10E-10 . . . 10E-3. Use %e printf placeholders to display your results in scientific notation. Define and call a function that describes the program's purpose to the user.

8. A manufacturer wishes to determine the cost of producing an open-top cylindrical container. The surface area of the container is the sum of the area of the circular base plus the area of the outside (the circumference of the base times the height of the container). Write a program to take the radius of the base, the height of the container, the cost per square centimeter of the material (cost), and the number of containers to be produced (quantity). Calculate the cost of each container and the total cost of producing all the containers. Write and call a function that displays instructions to the user.

CHAPTER 4

Selection Structures:
if and switch
Statements

QUICK-CHECK EXERCISES

1. An `if` statement implements _____ execution.
2. What is a compound statement?
3. A `switch` statement is often used instead of _____.
4. What can be the values of an expression with a relational operator?
5. The relational operator <= means _____.
6. A hand trace is used to verify that a(n) _____ is correct.
7. List the three types of control structures.
8. Correct the syntax errors.

```
if x > 25.0 {
      y = x
else
      y = z;
}
```

9. What value is assigned to `fee` by the `if` statement when `speed` is 75?

```
if (speed > 35)
      fee = 20.0;
else if (speed > 50)
      fee = 40.00;
else if (speed > 75)
      fee = 60.00;
```

10. Answer Exercise 9 for the `if` statement that follows. Which `if` statement seems reasonable?

```
if (speed > 75)
      fee = 60.0;
else if (speed > 50)
      fee = 40.00;
else if (speed > 35)
      fee = 20.00;
```

11. What output line(s) are displayed by the statements that follow when `grade` is `'I'`? When `grade` is `'B'`? When `grade` is `'b'`?

```
switch (grade) {
case 'A':
      points = 4;
      break;

case 'B':
      points = 3;
      break;

case 'C':
      points = 2;
      break;

case 'D':
      points = 1;
      break;

case 'E':
case 'I':
case 'W':
      points = 0;
}

if (points > 0)
      printf("Passed, points earned = %d\n", points);
else
      printf("Failed, no points earned\n");
```

12. Explain the difference between the statements on the left and the statements on the right. For each group of statements, give the final value of x if the initial value of x is 1.

```
if (x >= 0)                    if (x >= 0)
     x = x + 1;                    x = x + 1;
else if (x >= 1)               if (x >= 1)
     x = x + 2;                    x = x + 2;
```

13. a. Evaluate the expression

```
1  &&  (30 % 10 >= 0)  &&  (30 % 10 <= 3)
```

   b. Is either set of parentheses required?
   c. Write the complement of the expression two ways. First, add one operator and one set of parentheses. For the second version, use DeMorgan's theorem.

ANSWERS TO QUICK-CHECK EXERCISES

1. conditional
2. one or more statements surrounded by braces
3. nested `if` statements or a multiple-alternative `if` statement
4. 0 and 1
5. less than or equal to
6. algorithm
7. sequence, selection, repetition
8. Parenthesize condition, remove braces (or add them around `else`: `} else {}`, and add a semicolon to the first assignment statement.
9. 20.00 (first condition is met)
10. 40.00, the one in 10
11. when grade is `'I'`:
        Failed, no points earned
    when grade is `'B'`:
        Passed, points earned = 3
    when grade is `'b'`:
        The `switch` statement is skipped so the output printed depends on the previous value of `points` (which may be garbage).
12. A nested `if` statement is on the left; a sequence of `if` statements is on the right. On the left x becomes 2; on the right x becomes 4.
13. a. 1
    b. no
    c. `!(1  &&  (30 % 10 >= 0)  &&  (30 % 10 <= 3))`
       `0  ||  (30 % 10 < 0)  ||  (30 % 10 > 3)`

REVIEW QUESTIONS

1. Making a decision between two alternative courses of action is usually implemented with a(n) _____ statement in C.
2. Trace the following program fragment; indicate which function will be called if a data value of 27.34 is entered.

```
printf("Enter a temperature> ");
scanf("%lf", &temp);
if (temp > 32.0)
        not_freezing();
else
        ice_forming();
```

3. Write a multiple-alternative if statement to display a message based on the level of force, in newtons, being applied by a robot hand attempting to turn a large threaded part into a machine. Force levels and associated messages are: 0, Part not found; 1–44, Insecure grip; 45–88, Nominal grip; 89–100, Part may be misaligned; and above 100, DANGER--Part may be stuck. Print a message to indicate bad data as well.
4. Write a switch statement to select an operation based on the color of a sample observed by an automated chemical-flow control system that is checking to see whether material flowing into a processing vat is acidic or basic. If the color is indicated as 'B' (for blue), add to the total_bases variable the value of the variable base_strength. If the color is indicated as 'R' (for red), increase the value of the variable total_acids by the value of acid_strength. If the color is 'P' (for purple), add to the variable neutrals the value of sample_size. Do nothing if the color is 'Y' (for yellow). Display an error message if the value of color is not one of these four values.
5. Write an if statement that displays an acceptance message for an astronaut candidate if the person's weight is between the values of opt_min and opt_max inclusive, the person's age is between age_min and age_max inclusive, and the person is a nonsmoker (smoker is false).
6. Implement the flow diagram in Fig. 4.11 using a nested if structure.

PROGRAMMING PROJECTS

1. A pharmaceutical engineer is testing out new types of synthetic antibiotics that should kill either one or both of the common classes of bacteria, *gram-negative* and *gram-positive* bacteria. Depending on the type of bacteria killed in a sample, the engineer wants to leave different lists of instructions for a technician who will perform follow-up tests. Write a program that takes as input a character indicating whether an antibiotic sample is effective against only gram-negative bacteria ('N'), only gram-positive bacteria ('P'), both classes ('B'), or neither class ('Z'). The program displays different lists of instructions to a technician based on effectiveness against gram-positive and gram-negative bacteria:

```
Gram-positive: Perform standard tests 1 and 5.
               Record results in notebook #2.
```

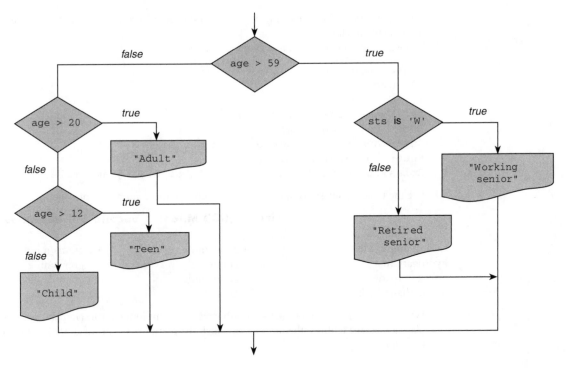

Figure 4.11 Flow Diagram for Review Question 6

```
Gram-negative: Perform standard tests 2, 3, and 4.
               Record results in notebook #3.
```

For samples effective on both classes, the program displays both sets of instructions. For samples effective on neither, the program displays Throw away sample.

Your program should define and call two functions—one to display the gram-positive instructions and one for the gram-negative instructions.

2. Write a program to simulate a state police radar gun. The program should take an automobile speed and display the message speeding if the speed exceeds 65 mph.

3. The National Earthquake Information Center has asked you to write a program implementing the following decision table to characterize an earthquake based on its Richter scale number.

Richter Scale Number (n)	Characterization
$n < 5.0$	Little or no damage
$5.0 \leq n < 5.5$	Some damage
$5.5 \leq n < 6.5$	Serious damage: walls may crack or fall
$6.5 \leq n < 7.5$	Disaster: houses and buildings may collapse
higher	Catastrophe: most buildings destroyed

Could you handle this problem with a `switch` statement? If so, use a `switch` statement; if not, explain why.

4. Write a program that interacts with the user like this:

```
(1) Carbon monoxide
(2) Hydrocarbons
(3) Nitrogen oxides
(4) Nonmethane hydrocarbons
Enter pollutant number>> 2
Enter number of grams emitted per mile>> 0.35
Enter odometer reading>> 40112
Emissions exceed permitted level of 0.31 grams/mile.
```

Use the table of emissions limits below to determine the appropriate message.[1]

	First 50,000 Miles	**Second 50,000 Miles**
carbon monoxide	3.4 grams/mile	4.2 grams/mile
hydrocarbons	0.31 grams/mile	0.39 grams/mile
nitrogen oxides	0.4 grams/mile	0.5 grams/mile
nonmethane hydrocarbons	0.25 grams/mile	0.31 grams/mile

5. Write a program that takes the x–y coordinates of a point in the Cartesian plane and displays a message telling either an axis on which the point lies or the quadrant in which it is found.

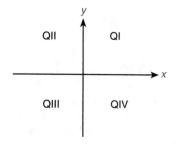

Sample lines of output:

```
(-1.0, -2.5) is in quadrant III
(0.0, 4.8) is on the y axis
```

6. Write a program that reports the contents of a compressed-gas cylinder based on the first letter of the cylinder's color. The program input is a character representing the observed color of the cylinder: `'Y'` or `'y'` for yellow, `'O'` or `'o'` for orange, and so on. Cylinder colors and associated contents are as follows:

---

[1]Adapted from Joseph Priest, *Energy: Principles, Problems, Alternatives* (Reading, MA.: Addison-Wesley, 1991), p. 164.

orange	ammonia
brown	carbon monoxide
yellow	hydrogen
green	oxygen

7. Los Angeles sometimes has very smoggy conditions. These conditions are largely due to L.A.'s location between mountain ranges, coupled with prevailing winds off the ocean that tend to blow pollutants from the city's many automobiles up against the mountains. Three components of smog—ozone, nitrogen dioxide, and carbon monoxide—are a particular health concern. A pollutant hazard index has been developed for each of the three primary irritants. If any index rises above 100, the air is listed as "unhealthful" in forecasts to Los Angeles residents. If the index for any one of the three rises above 200, a "first-stage smog alert" is issued and certain activities are restricted in the affected part of the Los Angeles basin. If an index goes over 275, a "second-stage alert" is called and more severe restrictions apply. Write a program that takes as input the daily hazard index for each of the three pollutants and that identifies unhealthful or first- or second-stage alert situations.

8. Engineers frequently must provide solutions based on imperfect or incomplete information. This is particularly true when dealing with somewhat subjective quantities, as one does when calculating risk-benefit trade-offs of a new technology. Assume that you are designing a study to decide which of several types of power plants is preferable to build in an area. You are to consider the following factors:

pollution_production	the pollutants generated by the plant
damage_risk	the risk of damage to neighboring the property if the plant explodes
cost_per_kwh	the cost per kilowatt hour for the electricity generated by the plant

To perform your study, you are going to develop a cost function:

$$cost = \frac{w1 \times pollution\_production}{MAX\_POLLUTION} + \frac{w2 \times damage\_risk}{MAX\_DAMAGE} + \frac{w3 \times cost\_per\_kwh}{MAX\_COST}$$

Write a program that allows a user to input values for *pollution_production*, *damage_risk*, and *cost_per_kwh* along with the three weighting values, *w1, w2,* and *w3.* Your program should display the *cost* for that user of the plant based on the inputs. Assume that the maximum units of pollutants that could be produced per kwh (*MAX_POLLUTION*) is 10, that the maximum number of households that could be displaced or damaged in an accident (*MAX_DAMAGE*) is 30,000, and that the maximum cost per kilowatt hour (*MAX_COST*) is $0.25. If the user weights one factor significantly higher (e.g., double or more) than both of the other values, the program should output a message following the cost display, suggesting that the user might like to run the program again using a lower value for that variable to obtain a comparison cost.

CHAPTER 5

Repetition and Loop Statements

QUICK-CHECK EXERCISES

1. A loop that continues to process input data until a special value is entered is called a
   _____-controlled loop.
2. Some `for` loops cannot be rewritten in C using a `while` loop. True or false?
3. It is an error if the body of a `for` loop never executes. True or false?
4. In an endfile-controlled `for` loop, the initialization and update expressions typically include calls to the function _____.
5. In a typical counter-controlled loop, the number of loop repetitions may not be known until the loop is executing. True or false?
6. During execution of the following program segment, how many lines of asterisks are displayed?

```
for  (i = 0;  i < 10;  ++i)
    for  (j = 0;  j < 5;  ++j)
        printf("**********\n");
```

7. During execution of the following program segment:

   a. How many times does the first call to `printf` execute?
   b. How many times does the second call to `printf` execute?
   c. What is the last value displayed?

```
for  (i = 0;  i < 7;  ++i) {
    for  (j = 0;  j < i;  ++j)
        printf("%4d", i * j);
    printf("\n");
}
```

8. If the value of n is 4 and m is 5, is the value of the following expression 21?

```
++(n * m)
```

Explain your answer.

9. What are the values of n, m, and p after execution of this three-statement fragment?

```
n = j - ++k;
m = j-- + k--;
p = k + j;
```

10. What are the values of x, y, and z after execution of this three-statement fragment?

```
x *= y + z;
y /= 2 * z + 1;
z += x;
```

11. What does the following code segment display? Try each of these inputs: 345, 82, 6. Then, describe the action of the code.

```
printf("\nEnter a positive integer> ");
scanf("%d", &num);
do {
     printf("%d   ", num % 10);
     num /= 10;
} while (num > 0);
printf("\n");
```

ANSWERS TO QUICK-CHECK EXERCISES

1. sentinel
2. false
3. false
4. fscanf
5. false
6. 50
7. a. 0 + 1 + 2 + 3 + 4 + 5 + 6 = 21
   b. 7
   c. 30
8. No. The expression is illegal. The increment operator cannot be applied to an expression such as (n * m).
9. n=2, m=8, p=6
10. x=21, y=1, z=23

11. Enter a positive integer> 345
    5 4 3
    Enter a positive integer> 82
    2 8
    Enter a positive integer> 6
    6

The code displays the digits of an integer in reverse order and separated by spaces.

REVIEW QUESTIONS

1. In what ways are the initialization, repetition test, and update steps alike for a sentinel-controlled loop and an endfile-controlled loop? How are they different?
2. Write a program that computes and displays the sum of a collection of Celsius temperatures entered at the terminal until a sentinel value of −275 is entered.
3. Hand trace the program that follows given the following data:

```
4 2 8 4    1 4 2 1    9 3 3 1    -22 10 8 2    3 3 4 5
```

```c
#include <stdio.h>
#define SPECIAL_SLOPE  0.0

int
main(void)
{
      double slope, y2, y1, x2, x1;

      printf("Enter 4 numbers separated by spaces.");
      printf("\nThe last two numbers cannot be the ");
      printf("same, but\nthe program terminates if ");
      printf("the first two are.\n");
      printf("\nEnter four numbers> ");
      scanf("%lf%lf%lf%lf", &y2, &y1, &x2, &x1);

      for (slope = (y2 - y1) / (x2 - x1);
           slope != SPECIAL_SLOPE;
           slope = (y2 - y1) / (x2 - x1)) {
         printf("Slope is %5.2f.\n", slope);
         printf("\nEnter four more numbers> ");
         scanf("%lf%lf%lf%lf", &y2, &y1, &x2, &x1);
      }
      return (0);
}
```

4. Rewrite the program in Review Question 3 so it uses a while loop.

5. Rewrite the program segment that follows, using a `for` loop:

```
count = 0;
i = 0;
while (i < n) {
    scanf("%d", &x);
    if (x == i)
            ++count;
    ++i;
}
```

6. Rewrite this `for` loop heading, omitting any invalid semicolons.

```
for (i = n;
     i < max;
     ++i;);
```

7. Write a `do-while` loop that repeatedly prompts for and takes input until a value in the range 0 through 15 inclusive is input. Include code that prevents the loop from cycling indefinitely on input of a wrong data type.

PROGRAMMING PROJECTS

1. The rate of decay of a radioactive isotope is given in terms of its half-life H, the time lapse required for the isotope to decay to one-half of its original mass. The isotope strontium 90 (Sr^{90}) has a half-life of 28 years. Compute and display in table form the amount of this isotope that remains after each year for n years, given the initial presence of an amount in grams. The values of n and *amount* should be provided interactively. The amount of Sr^{90} remaining can be computed by using the following formula:

$$r = amount \times C^{(y/H)}$$

where *amount* is the initial amount in grams, C is expressed as $e^{-0.693}$ ($e = 2.71828$), y is the number of years elapsed, and H is the half-life of the isotope in years.

2. The value for π can be determined by the series equation

$$\pi = 4 \times \left(1 - \frac{1}{3} + \frac{1}{5} - \frac{1}{7} + \frac{1}{9} - \frac{1}{11} + \frac{1}{13} - \dots \right)$$

Write an interactive program that asks the user how many terms of the series equation to use in approximating π. Then calculate and display the approximation. Here is a sample run:

```
Pi Approximation Program

How many terms of the series should be included?
(The more terms, the better the approximation.)
=> 3
Approximate value of pi is 3.4667
```

3. Write a program that finds the equivalent series and parallel resistance for a collection of resistor values. Your program should scan first the number of resistors and then the resistor values. Then compute the equivalent series resistance for all resistors in the collection and also the equivalent parallel resistance. For example, if there are three resistors of 100, 200, and 300 ohms, respectively, their equivalent series resistance is 100 + 200 + 300 and their equivalent parallel resistance is

$$\cfrac{1}{\cfrac{1}{100} + \cfrac{1}{200} + \cfrac{1}{300}}$$

After your program works for a single collection of resistors, modify it so it can process several collections of resistors in a single run. Use a sentinel value of 0 (zero resistors in the collection) to signal the end of the program data.

4. Manufacturing engineers use three principal measures of the roughness of the surface of an object. All are based on measurements at evenly spaced intervals along the surface as diagrammed here and labeled a, b, c, ...

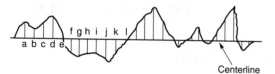

Figure from Serope Kalpakjian, *Manufacturing Engineering and Technology,* 3rd ed. (Reading, Mass.: Addison-Wesley, 1995), p. 962.

Values above the centerline are positive; values below are negative. The three roughness indicators are:

Arithmetic mean value (R_a):

$$R_a = \frac{|a| + |b| + |c| + \cdots}{n}$$

Root-mean-square average (R_q):

$$R_q = \sqrt{\frac{a^2 + b^2 + c^2 + \cdots}{n}}$$

Maximum roughness height:
    height from level of deepest trough to highest peak

Write a program that takes surface measurements from the file `surface.dat` and computes and displays these three surface roughness indicators.

Sample file `surface.dat`

```
-4.1 -2.2 -0.5 1.2 3.3 4.6 5.1 2.1 0.2 -3.6 -4.1  0.2 0.5 2.2 4.1
-0.2 -1.2 -3.3 -4.6 -5.0 -2.2  -1.1 0.8 3.2 -0.1 -4.8
```

5. When an object radiating light or other energy moves toward or away from an observer, the radiation will seem to shift in frequency. This phenomenon, called the *Doppler shift*, is frequently used in measuring indirectly the velocity or changes in velocity of an object or weather pattern relative to an observer. For example, a weather radar that attempts to find dangerous wind shear near airports relies on this phenomenon.

   For a radar transmitting at frequency f_t, the difference in transmitting and received frequencies due to a target moving at speed v (m/s) relative to the radar—that is, directly toward or away from the radar—is given by

$$\frac{f_r - f_t}{f_t} = \frac{2v}{c}$$

A thunderstorm approaches in the Wyoming high country.
(Courtesy of Professor Robert D. Kelly, University of Wyoming, Department of Atmospheric Science.)

where f_r is the received frequency and c is the speed of light (3×10^8 m/s). A weather service station at a major municipal airport is using a C-band Doppler radar (f_t = 5.5 GHz). During a severe thunderstorm, the following received frequencies are observed:

Time (s)	Frequency (GHz)
0	5.500000040
100	5.500000095
200	5.500000230
300	5.500001800
400	5.500000870
500	5.500000065
600	5.500000370

Write a program that scans this data and displays a table showing the data along with a third column displaying the Doppler velocities of the winds relative to the radar. What would happen if all the winds in the storm were moving perpendicular to the radar beam?

6. The greatest common divisor (gcd) of two integers is the product of the integers' common factors. Write a program that inputs two numbers and implements the following approach to finding their gcd. We will use the numbers –252 and 735. Working with the numbers' absolute values, we find the remainder of one divided by the other.

$$
\begin{array}{r}
0 \\
735\overline{\smash)252} \\
0 \\
\hline
252
\end{array}
$$

Now we calculate the remainder of the old divisor divided by the remainder found.

$$
\begin{array}{r}
2 \\
252\overline{\smash)735} \\
504 \\
\hline
231
\end{array}
$$

We repeat this process until the remainder is zero.

$$
\begin{array}{r}
1 \\
231\overline{\smash)252} \\
231 \\
\hline
21
\end{array}
\qquad
\begin{array}{r}
11 \\
21\overline{\smash)231} \\
21 \\
21 \\
21 \\
\hline
0
\end{array}
$$

The last divisor (21) is the gcd.

7. An integer n is divisible by 9 if the sum of its digits is divisible by 9. Use the algorithm developed for Project 6, and write a program to determine whether or not the following numbers are divisible by 9.

154368   621594   123456

8. The pressure of a gas changes as the volume and temperature of the gas vary. Write a program that uses the Van der Waals equation of state for a gas,

$$\left(P + \frac{an^2}{V^2}\right)(V - bn) = nRT$$

to display in tabular form the relationship between the pressure and the volume of n moles of carbon dioxide at a constant absolute temperature (T). P is the pressure in atmospheres and V is the volume in liters. The Van der Waals constants for carbon dioxide are $a = 3.592$ $L^2 \cdot$ atm/mol^2 and $b = 0.0427$ L/mol. Use 0.08206 L $\cdot$ atm/mol $\cdot$ K for the gas constant R. Inputs to the program include n, the Kelvin temperature, the initial and final volumes in milliliters, and the volume increment between lines of the table. Your program will display a table that varies the volume of the gas from the initial to the final volume in steps prescribed by the volume increment. Here is a sample run:

```
Please enter at the prompts the number of moles of
carbon dioxide, the absolute temperature, the initial
volume in  milliliters, the final volume, and the
increment volume between lines of the table.

Quantity of carbon dioxide (moles)> 0.02
Temperature (kelvin)> 300
Initial volume (milliliters)> 400
Final volume (milliliters)> 600
Volume increment (milliliters)> 50

0.0200 moles of carbon dioxide at 300 kelvin

Volume (ml)          Pressure (atm)

   400                  1.2246
   450                  1.0891
   500                  0.9807
   550                  0.8918
   600                  0.8178
```

9. A concrete channel to bring water to Crystal Lake is being designed. It will have vertical walls and be 15 feet wide. It will be 10 feet deep, have a slope of .0015 feet/foot, and have a roughness coefficient of .014. How deep will the water be when 1000 cubic feet per second is flowing through the channel?

To solve this problem, we can use Manning's equation

$$Q = \frac{1.486}{N}AR^{2/3}S^{1/2}$$

where Q is the flow of water (cubic feet per second), N is the roughness coefficient (unitless), A is the area (square feet), S is the slope (feet/foot), and R is the hydraulic radius (feet).

The hydraulic radius is the cross-sectional area divided by the wetted perimeter. For square channels like the one in this example,

Hydraulic radius = depth × width / (2.0 × depth + width)

To solve this problem, design a program that allows the user to guess a depth and then calculates the corresponding flow. If the flow is too little, the user should guess a depth a little higher; if the flow is too high, the user should guess a depth a little lower. The guessing is repeated until the computed flow is within 0.1 percent of the flow desired.

To help the user make an initial guess, the program should display the flow for half the channel depth. Note the example run:

```
At a depth of 5.0000 feet, the flow is 641.3255 cubic
feet per second.

Enter your initial guess for the channel depth
when the flow is 1000.0000 cubic feet per second
Enter guess> 6.0

Depth: 6.0000  Flow: 825.5906 cfs  Target: 1000.0000 cfs
Difference: 174.4094  Error: 17.4409 percent

Enter guess> 7.0

Depth: 7.0000  Flow: 1017.7784 cfs  Target: 1000.0000 cfs
Difference: -17.7784  Error: -1.7778 percent

Enter guess> 6.8
. . .
```

10. The Environmental Awareness Club of BigCorp, Int'l. is proposing that the company subsidize at $.08 per passenger km the commuting costs of employees who form carpools that meet a prescribed minimum passenger efficiency. Passenger efficiency P (in passenger · k/L) is defined as

$$P = \frac{ns}{l}$$

where n is the number of passengers, s is the distance traveled in km, and l is the number of liters of gasoline used.

Write a program that prompts the user for a minimum passenger efficiency and then processes a file of data on existing carpools (`carpool.dat`), displaying a table of all carpools that meet the passenger efficiency minimum. The file represents each carpool as a data line containing three numbers: the number of people in the carpool, the total commuting distance per five-day week, and the number of liters of gasoline consumed in a week of commuting. The data file ends with a line of zeros. Display your results in a table with this format:

```
CARPOOLS MEETING MINIMUM PASSENGER EFFICIENCY OF 25 PASSENGER KM / L

Passengers    Weekly Commute      Gasoline        Efficiency        Weekly
                 (km)          Consumption(L)    (pass km / L)     Subsidy($)
    4             75               11.0              27.3            24.00
    2             60                4.5              26.7             9.60
   . . .
```

CHAPTER 6

Modular Programming

QUICK-CHECK EXERCISES

1. The items passed in a function call are the _____ _____. The corresponding _____ _____ appear in the function heading.

2. Constants and expressions can be actual arguments corresponding to formal parameters that are _____ parameters.

3. Formal parameters that are output parameters must have actual arguments that are _____.

4. If an actual argument of -35.7 is passed to a type int formal parameter, what will happen?

5. If an actual argument of 17 is passed to a type double formal parameter, what will happen?

6. Which of the following is used to test a function: a driver or a stub?

7. Which of the following is used to test program flow in a partially complete system: a driver or a stub?

8. What are the values of main function variables x and y at the point marked /* values here */ in the following program?

```
void silly(int x);

int
main(void)
```

```
{
        int x, y;

        x = 10; y = 11;
        silly(x);
        silly(y);    /* values here */
            . . .
}

/* nonsense */
void
silly(int x)
{
        int y;

        y = x + 2;
        x *= 2;
}
```

9. Let's make some changes in our nonsense program. What are main's x and y at /*
    values here */ in this version?

```
void silly(int *x);

int
main(void)
{
        int x, y;

        x = 10;    y = 11;
        silly(&x);
        silly(&y);    /* values here */
            . . .
}
/* nonsense */
void
silly(int *x)
{
        int y;
        y = *x + 2;
        *x *= 2;
}
```

10. What problem do you notice in the following recursive function? Show two possible
    ways to correct the problem.

```
int
silly(int n)
{
        if (n <= 0)
                return (1);
```

```
          else if (n % 2 == 0)
                  return (n);
          else
                  silly(n - 3);
      }
```

11. What is a common cause of a stack overflow error?
12. What can you say about a recursive algorithm that has the following form?

    if condition
        Perform recursive step.

ANSWERS TO QUICK-CHECK EXERCISES

1. actual arguments; formal parameters
2. input
3. addresses of variables/ pointers
4. The formal parameter's value will be -35.
5. The formal parameter's value will be 17.0.
6. Driver
7. Stub
8. x is 10, y is 11
9. x is 20, y is 22
10. One path through the function does not encounter a return statement. Either place a return statement in the final else

    ```
    return (silly(n - 3));
    ```

    or assign 1, n, silly(n-3) to a local variable, and place that variable in a return statement at the end of the function.
11. Too many recursive calls
12. Nothing is done when the simplest case is reached.

REVIEW QUESTIONS

1. Write the prototype for a function called script that has three input parameters. The first parameter will be the number of spaces to display at the beginning of a line. The second parameter will be the character to display after the spaces, and the third parameter will be the number of times to display the second parameter on the same line.
2. Write a function called letter_grade that has a type int parameter called points and returns the appropriate letter grade using a straight scale (90 – 100 is an A, 80 – 89 is a B, and so on).
3. Why would you choose to write a function that computes a single numeric or character value as a nonvoid function that returns a result through a return statement rather than to write a void function with an output parameter?

4. Explain the allocation of memory cells when a function is called.
5. Which of the functions in the following program outline *can* call the function grumpy? All prototypes and declarations are shown; only executable statements are omitted.

```
int grumpy(int dopey);
char silly(double grumpy);
double happy(int goofy, char greedy);

int
main(void)
{
        double p,q,r;
        . . .
}

int
grumpy(int dopey)
{
        double silly;
        . . .
}

char
silly(double grumpy)
{
        double happy;
        . . .
}

double
happy(int goofy, char greedy)
{
        char grumpy;
        . . .
}
```

6. Sketch the data areas of functions main and silly as they appear immediately before the return from the first call to silly in Quick-Check Exercise 9.
7. Present arguments against these statements:
   a. It is foolish to use function subprograms because a program written with functions has many more lines than the same program written without functions.
   b. The use of function subprograms leads to more errors because of mistakes in using argument lists.

PROGRAMMING PROJECTS

1. Write a function that rounds a number to a given number of decimal places and returns the rounded value as the function result.

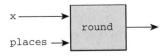

For example, the call round(7.8257, 2) would return the value 7.83. (*Hint:* To round a number to the nearest integer, add 0.5 and then truncate the sum, discarding the fractional part.)

$$
\begin{array}{r}
782.57 \\
+\ .5 \\
\hline
783.0\cancel{07}
\end{array}
$$

Write a driver function that prompts the user for a number and then repeatedly calls the function and displays the number rounded to four decimal places, then three places, then two, then one, then zero decimal places. For example,

```
Enter a value=> 7.8257
     7.8257
     7.8260
     7.8300
     7.8000
     8.0000
```

2. Write a function named `factor` that factors its parameter, displaying the parameter and all its prime factors. For example, the function call `factor(84)` should display

$$
84 = 2 \times 2 \times 3 \times 7
$$

(*Hint:* Use function `find_div` from Fig. 6.13. Write a driver that tests your function with prime numbers and also with numbers having from two to eight prime factors.)

3. Two positive integers i and j are considered to be *relatively prime* if there exists no integer greater than 1 that divides them both. Write a function `relprm` that has two input parameters, i and j, and returns a value of 1 for true if and only if i and j are relatively prime. Otherwise, `relprm` should return a value of 0 for false.

4. Given the lengths *a*, *b*, *c* of the sides of a triangle, write a function to compute the area *A* of the triangle. The formula for computing *A* is given by

$$
A = \sqrt{s(s-a)\,(s-b)\,(s-c)}
$$

where *s* is the semiperimeter of the triangle

$$
s = \frac{a+b+c}{2}
$$

Write a driver program to get values for a, b, and c and call your function to compute A. The driver should display A, a, b, and c.

5. The square root of a number N can be approximated by repeated calculation using the formula

$$NG = 0.5(LG + N/LG)$$

where NG stands for next guess and LG stands for last guess. Write a function that calculates the square root of a number using this method.

The initial guess will be the starting value of LG. The program will compute a value for NG using the formula given. The difference between NG and LG is checked to see whether these two guesses are almost identical. If they are, NG is accepted as the square root; otherwise, the new guess (NG) becomes the last guess (LG) and the process is repeated (another value is computed for NG, the difference is checked, and so on). The loop should be repeated until the difference is less than 0.005. Use an initial guess of 1.0.

Write a driver function and test your square root function for the numbers 4, 120.5, 88, 36.01, and 10000.

6. When an aircraft or an automobile is moving through the atmosphere, it must overcome a force called *drag* that works against the motion of the vehicle. The drag force can be expressed as

$$F = \frac{1}{2} CD \times A \times \rho \times V^2$$

where F is the force (in newtons), CD is the drag coefficient, A is the projected area of the vehicle perpendicular to the velocity vector (in m²), ρ is the density of the gas or fluid through which the body is traveling (kg/m³), and V is the body's velocity. The drag coefficient CD has a complex derivation and is frequently an empirical quantity. Sometimes the drag coefficient has its own dependencies on velocities: For an automobile, the range is from approximately 0.2 (for a very streamlined vehicle) through about 0.5. For simplicity, assume a streamlined passenger vehicle is moving through air at sea level (where $\rho = 1.23$ kg/m³). Write a program that allows a user to input A and CD interactively and calls a function to compute the drag force. Your program should display a table showing the drag force for the input shape for a range of velocities from 0 m/s to 40 m/s.

7. Write a function `ln_approx` that computes an approximation of the natural logarithm of a number between 1 and 2 by summing a given number of terms of this series:

$$\ln(1 + x) = \sum_{n=1}^{\infty} \frac{(-1)^{n+1} x^n}{n}$$

Also, write a driver that calls `ln_approx` twice with the same value, requesting first the sum of four terms of the series and then requesting seven terms. The program should display a message comparing the results of the two calls to the value returned by the math library function `log`.

8. A control system applies a force to an actuator proportional to the voltage of a signal coming into the control system. It is desired not to allow the actuator to quiver back and forth in the presence of small corrections near the zero-force point. More force is required for the actuator to move to the left (negative direction of motion) than is required for motion to the right (positive direction of motion.) Assume that the transfer function (the relationship between the voltage and the movement) of the actuator is

- Voltage less than –0.2 volt: Actuator moves 1 cm/volt in the negative direction
- Absolute value of voltage less than or equal to 0.2 volt: No motion
- Voltage greater than 0.2 volt: Actuator moves 2 cm/volt in the positive direction.

Write a function to compute the total motion for any single signal input. Write a main function that repeatedly calls the motion calculation function using an input signal stream such as this: –10.0 v, –8.0 v, –0.21 v, –0.20 v, –0.05 v, 1.5 v, 0.00 v, 4.5 v. The main function should also take as user input an initial position of the actuator and should output a final position resulting from applying the signals of the given control stream. For one test, simulate the effect of the given voltages for an initial position of 1.5 cm to find the final position of the actuator.

9. Use the recursive bisection function from Fig. 6.30 and a variant of function $f(\theta)$ from the "Roots of Equations" introduction in a program to approximate the necessary angle of elevation (radians) at which to launch a projectile traveling 250 m/s in order to impact a target 3300 m away at a height of 3 m. The approximation should be within 0.00001 of the actual angle. Use $g = 9.81$ m/s² as the gravitational acceleration. Your program should repeatedly prompt the user to enter endpoints of subintervals of the interval $[0, \pi/2]$ radians until an interval is entered that contains an odd number of roots of f. Then call bisect with this interval and display the root returned.

CHAPTER 7

Arrays

1. What is a data structure?
2. Of what data type are array subscripting expressions?
3. Can two elements of the same array be of different data types?
4. If an array is declared to have ten elements, must the program use all ten?
5. Let nums be an array of 12 type int locations. Describe how the following loop works.

```
i = 0;
for  (status = scanf("%d", &n);
       status == 1 && i < 12;
       status = scanf("%d", &n))
    nums[i++] = n;
```

Can you tell from this code fragment whether nums is an array allocated on the stack in a function data area or whether it is a pointer that accesses an array allocated on the heap?

6. An _____ loop allows us to access easily the elements of an array in sequential order.
7. What is the difference in the use of array b that is implied by these two headings?

```
int                        int
fun_one(int b[], n)        fun_two(const int b[], n)
```

8. Look again at the headings in Exercise 7. Why does neither array declaration indicate a size?
9. Which of the following strings could represent space allocated for a local variable? Which could represent a formal parameter of any length?

```
char str1[50]       char str2[]
```

10. A program you have written is producing incorrect results on your second data set, although it runs fine on the first. You discover after adding extra print statements for debugging that the value of one of your strings is spontaneously changing from "blue" to "al" in the following code segment. What could be wrong?

```
. . .
printf("%s\n", s1);  /*  displays "blue" */
scanf("%s", s2);
printf("%s\n", s1);  /*  displays "al"   */
. . .
```

11. Declare a variable str with as little space as would be reasonable given that str will hold each of the following values in turn:

```
carbon    uranium    tungsten    bauxite
```

12. If x is an array declared

```
int x[10];
```

and you see a function call such as

```
some_fun(x, n);
```

how can you tell whether x is an input or an output argument?

ANSWERS TO QUICK-CHECK EXERCISES

1. A data structure is a grouping of related values in main memory.
2. Type int
3. No
4. No
5. As long as scanf continues to return a value of 1 meaning a valid integer has been obtained for n, unless the subscript i is ≥ 12, the loop body will store the input in the next element of nums and will increment the loop counter. The loop exits on EOF (scanf returns a negative value), on invalid data (scanf returns zero), or on i no longer being less than 12. No, you can't tell.
6. indexed
7. In fun_one, b can be used as an output parameter or as an input/output parameter. In fun_two, b is strictly an input parameter array.
8. The size of b is not needed because the function does not allocate storage for copying parameter arrays. Only the starting address of the actual argument array will be stored in the formal parameter.
9. local variable: str1   parameter: str2
10. The call to scanf may be getting a string too long to fit in s2, and the extra characters could be overwriting memory allocated to s1.
11. char str[9] The longest value ("tungsten") has eight characters, and one more is needed for the null character.
12. You can't tell by looking at the function call, nor can you rely on the prototype of some_fun to tell you either unless the corresponding formal parameter declaration has a const qualifier. If it does, x must be an input argument.

REVIEW QUESTIONS

1. Identify an error in the following C statements:

```
int x[8], i;
for  (i = 0;  i <= 8;  ++i)
     x[i] = i;
```

Will the error be detected? If so, when?
2. Declare an array of type double values called exper that can be referenced by using any day of the week as a subscript where 0 represents Sunday, 1 represents Monday, and so on.
3. The statement marked /* this one */ in the following code is valid. True or false?

```
int counts[10], i;
double x[5];
printf("Enter an integer between 0 and 4> ");
i = 0;
scanf("%d", &counts[i]);
x[counts[i]] = 8.384;  /* this one */
```

4. Write a program segment that would make a copy of a string variable with the first occurrence of a specified letter deleted.
5. Write a C program segment to display the indexes of the smallest and the largest numbers in an array x of 20 integers. Assume array x already has values assigned to each element.
6. Write a C function called reverse that takes an array named x as an input parameter and an array named y as an output parameter. A third function parameter is n, the number of values in x. The function should copy the integers in x into y but in reverse order (i.e., y[0] gets x[n - 1], . . . y[n - 1] gets x[0]).

PROGRAMMING PROJECTS

1. Modems transmit computer data across phone lines. To do so, they convert sequences of zeros and ones, the binary numbers that are used for data representation in a digital computer, to analog signals of two frequencies. A calling modem transmits each data bit 1 as a 1270-hertz tone lasting one time unit and each data bit 0 as a 1070-hertz tone. Write a function that displays messages indicating the tones that would be emitted for the data represented by the function's string argument, a string of the characters zero and one. The messages should take the form

```
Emit ___-hz tone for ___ time unit(s).
```

where the tone frequency changes in each message. For example, if the argument were the string "100001101011110001", your function would display

```
Emit 1270-hz tone for 1 time unit(s).
Emit 1070-hz tone for 4 time unit(s).
Emit 1270-hz tone for 2 time unit(s).
Emit 1070-hz tone for 1 time unit(s).
Emit 1270-hz tone for 1 time unit(s).
Emit 1070-hz tone for 1 time unit(s).
Emit 1270-hz tone for 4 time unit(s).
Emit 1070-hz tone for 3 time unit(s).
Emit 1270-hz tone for 1 time unit(s).
```

2. Write a program to take two numerical lists of the same length ended by a sentinel value and store the lists in arrays x and y, each of which has 20 elements. Let n be the actual number of data values in each list. Store the product of corresponding elements of x and y in a third array, z, also of size 20. Display the arrays x, y, and z in a three-column table. Then compute and display the square root of the sum of the items in z. Make up your own data, and be sure to test your program on at least one data set with number lists of exactly

20 items. One data set should have lists of 21 numbers, and one set should have significantly shorter lists.

3. Healthfair Pharmaceuticals runs a continual color and opacity quality check on its liquid-antibiotic production line. The test is performed by shining a laser through each vial on the production line and recording how much light is detected on the far side of the vial. The following statistics are needed for each 30-vial batch of antibiotics: the average (mean) light absorptivity of the vials of antibiotics, the variance, and the standard deviation of the absorptivity data. The formula for standard deviation shown in Section 7.3 represents the standard deviation of a population. Since this quality-check problem does not call for computing the standard deviation of absorptivity data for the entire population of Healthfair antibiotics, but only the standard deviation of a 30-vial sample, use this slightly different formula for the standard deviation of a sample of size n:

$$Standard\ deviation = \sqrt{\frac{\sum_{i=0}^{n-1} (a[i] - mean)^2}{n-1}}$$

The absorptivity of the ith vial of antibiotics is $a[i]$. The variance is the square of the standard deviation. Write a program that computes the needed statistics for a stream of user-entered absorptivity data (values between 0 and 1).

4. Having spent a lot of time typing in C programs, you have resolved to invent a specialized new kind of keyboard to aid you. (There have been a variety of attempts to improve keyboards for standard typing applications, notably the "Dvorak keyboard.") In your product, you plan to place the most commonly used keys for C programming in the shortest finger-travel positions. You suspect that keys such as "*" and ";" are more commonly used in C programs than in English prose. However, before designing this keyboard, you need to get some hard data about the keys most commonly used in writing C source code.

Write a program that takes as input a C source code file, counts the number of occurrences of each keyboard character in the file, and writes the results to another file. Keep the count data in a one-dimensional array of integers, each element of which corresponds to the number of occurrences of one character. Recall that every character is represented by an integer character code. Assume that the possible character code range is 0–127. Write the characters found in the file and the number of times each character occurs, one entry per line. Hint: The character 'A' can be converted to its integer character code by using the cast (int) 'A', and the ASCII character code 65 can be converted to its character equivalent ('A') by using the cast (char)65.

5. Generate a table that indicates the rainfall for the city of Plainview and compares the current year's rainfall for the city with the rainfall from the previous year. Display summary statistics that will indicate both the annual rainfall for each year and the average monthly rainfall for each year. The input data will consist of twelve pairs of numbers. The first number in each pair will be the current year's rainfall for a month, and the second number will be what fell during the same month the previous year. The first data pair will represent January, the second will represent February, and so forth. If you assume the data begin

```
3.2   4     (for January)
2.2   1.6   (for February)
```

the output should resemble the following:

```
            Table of monthly rainfall

                 January     February    March . . .
This year          3.2         2.2
Last year          4.0         1.6

Total rainfall this year:  35.7
Total rainfall last year:  42.8
Average monthly rainfall for this year:  3.6
Average monthly rainfall for last year:  4.0
```

6. Write and test a function hydroxide that returns a 1 for true if its string argument ends in the substring OH.

   Try the function hydroxide on the following data:

   KOH   H2O2   NaCl   NaOH   C9H8O4   MgOH

7. Write a function that will merge the contents of two sorted (ascending order) arrays of type double values, storing the result in an array output parameter (still in ascending order). The function should not assume that both its input parameter arrays are the same length but can assume that one array does not contain two copies of the same value. The result array should also contain no duplicate values.

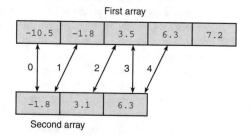

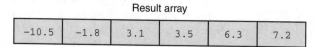

   Hint: When one of the input arrays has been exhausted, do not forget to copy the remaining data in the other array into the result array. Test your function with cases in which (1) the first array is exhausted first, (2) the second array is exhausted first, and (3) the two arrays are exhausted at the same time (i.e., they end with the same value). Remember that the arrays input to this function *must already be sorted*.

8. The binary search algorithm that follows may be used to search an array when the elements are in order. This algorithm is analogous to the following approach for finding a name in a telephone book.

   a. Open the book in the middle, and look at the middle name on the page.
   b. If the middle name isn't the one you're looking for, decide whether it comes before or after the name you want.

   c. Take the appropriate half of the section of the book you were looking in and repeat these steps until you land on the name.

Algorithm for Binary Search

1. Let `bottom` be the subscript of the initial array element.
2. Let `top` be the subscript of the last array element.
3. Let `found` be false.
4. Repeat as long as `bottom` isn't greater than `top` and the target has not been found
    5. Let `middle` be the subscript of the element halfway between `bottom` and `top`.
    6. if the element at `middle` is the target
        7. Set `found` to true and `index` to `middle`.
    else if the element at `middle` is larger than the target
        8. Let `top` be `middle` – 1.
    else
        9. Let `bottom` be `middle` + 1.

Write and test a function `binary_srch` that implements this algorithm for an array of integers. When there is a large number of array elements, which function do you think is faster: `binary_srch` or the linear search function of Fig. 7.13?

9. If n points are connected to form a closed polygon as shown below, the area A of the polygon can be calculated as

$$A = \frac{1}{2}\left|\sum_{i=0}^{n-2}(x_{i+1} + x_i)(y_{i+1} - y_i)\right|$$

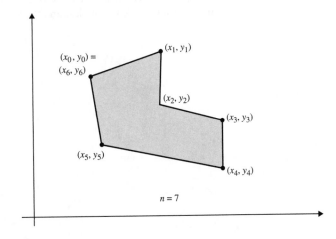

Notice that although the illustrated polygon has only six distinct corners, n for this polygon is 7 because the algorithm expects that the last point, (x_6, y_6), will be a repeat of the initial point, (x_0, y_0). Allocate parallel type double arrays x and y to hold coordinates of polygon corners. Define a function scan_polygon to fill the arrays from a file whose first line contains the value for n and then has n lines containing (x, y) coordinates represented as two numbers separated by a space. Define a function print_polygon that lists each (x, y) coordinate on a separate line (as a parenthesized pair of numbers separated by a comma), and a function polygon_area that returns the area of the polygon as its result.

For one test, use this data set, which defines a polygon whose area is 25.5 square units:

x	y
4	0
4	7.5
7	7.5
7	3
9	0
7	0
4	0

10. Many engineering applications require "normalizing" an n-element vector V. Each element w_i of the normalized unit vector W is defined as follows:

$$w_i = \frac{v_i}{\sqrt{\sum_{i=0}^{n-1} v_i^2}}$$

Write a program that inputs a vector of any length terminated by a sentinel value and displays both the original vector and a corresponding unit vector. Define and call a function normalize that takes an array input parameter and an array output parameter and stores in the output parameter the normalized version of the input parameter. Write a main function that thoroughly tests your class and the normalize function.

CHAPTER 8

Multidimensional Arrays

QUICK-CHECK EXERCISES

1. If m is a 5×5 integer matrix, what is displayed by this loop?

```
for  (i = 0;  i < 5;  ++i)
    printf("%8d", m[2][i]);
```

What is displayed by this loop?

```
for  (i = 0;  i < 5;  ++i)
    printf("%8d", m[i][4]);
```

2. Which of the arrays shown would be valid actual arguments to pass to a function whose prototype was

```
int fun(double arr[][3][10]);    ?
```

```
double m[6][3][10];
int n[4][3][10];
double z[8][2][11];
double q[20][3][10];
```

3. How many elements are in each of the arrays declared in Exercise 2?
4. Declare and initialize C arrays to represent the vector <4, 12, 19> and the matrix

$$\begin{bmatrix} 4.1 & 8.3 \\ 7.9 & 6.2 \end{bmatrix}$$

5. A matrix composed of the coefficients of a system of linear equations and of the vector of constants representing the right-hand side of the system is called a(n) _____ _____.

ANSWERS TO QUICK-CHECK EXERCISES

1. The middle row of m; the last column of m
2. Arrays m and q
3. m—180 elements; n—120 elements; z—176 elements; q—600 elements

4. ```
   int vect[3] = {4, 12, 19};
   double mat[2][2] = {{4.1, 8.3}, {7.9, 6.2}};
   ```

5. augmented matrix
   ```

REVIEW QUESTIONS

1. Identify an error in this C program fragment:

```
int     i, j;
double  grid[5][3];

for  (i = 0;  i < 5;  ++i)
    for  (j = 0;  j < 3;  ++j)
        printf("%.3f\n", grid[j][i]);
```

   How would you correct the error?

2. If sq is a C array representing the matrix

$$\begin{bmatrix} 4 & 5 & 18 \\ 2 & 4 & 9 \\ 8 & 4 & 12 \end{bmatrix}$$

   what is displayed by this code fragment?

```
for  (i = 0;  i < 3;  ++i)
    printf("%8d", sq[i][i]);
```

3. Is it possible to write a C function that can take as an argument either an array declared to be $5 \times 2 \times 3$ or an array declared to be $3 \times 2 \times 3$? Why or why not?

4. Write the augmented matrix that corresponds to the following system of equations:

$$2x_1 + x_2 - 4x_3 = -4$$
$$x_1 - 4x_2 + x_3 = -5$$
$$-x_1 + 3x_2 - 2x_3 = 1$$

5. Scale and triangularize the augmented matrix in Question 4. Then use back substitution to solve the system.

6. Write a program segment to display the sum of the values in each row of a 5×3 type double array named table. How many row sums will be displayed?

7. Answer Question 6 for the column sums.

PROGRAMMING PROJECTS

1. You have been asked to write one part of a detector analysis software package for a telescope. Your program takes as input the brightness of each point in a two-dimensional array representing an image of the sky. Use a 10×10 integer array for this image. Find and display the x and y coordinates and the value of the brightest pixel. If more than one pixel has this highest value, information for all highest-valued pixels should be displayed.

2. A robot that can rotate on a pedestal has a sensor that measures Cartesian coordinates (x', y') relative to the robot itself. It is desired, however, to know object coordinates (x, y) relative to the fixed coordinate system in which the robot rotates. If the robot is rotated counterclockwise through the angle θ relative to the fixed system,

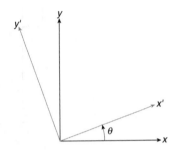

then coordinates in the fixed system are related to the robot's coordinate system by the following transformation:

$$\begin{bmatrix} x \\ y \end{bmatrix} = M \begin{bmatrix} x' \\ y' \end{bmatrix}$$

where M is the matrix

$$M = \begin{bmatrix} \cos\theta & -\sin\theta \\ \sin\theta & \cos\theta \end{bmatrix}$$

Write a program that takes positions in the (x', y') system (as measured by the sensor) and reports the equivalent coordinates in the fixed (x, y) coordinate system for user-input values of θ between 0 and π radians.

3. The *Game of Life*, invented by John H. Conway, is supposed to model the genetic laws for birth, survival, and death (see *Scientific American*, October 1970, p. 120). We will play the game on a board that consists of 25 squares in the horizontal and vertical directions (a total of 625 squares). Each square can be empty, or it can contain an X indicating the presence of an organism. Each square (except for the border squares) has eight neighbors. The color shading shown in the following segment of the board marks the neighbors of the organism named X*:

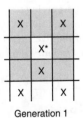

Generation 1

The next generation of organisms is determined according to the following criteria:
a. Birth—an organism will be born in each empty location that has exactly three neighbors.
b. Death—an organism with four or more organisms as neighbors will die from overcrowding. An organism with fewer than two neighbors will die from loneliness.
c. Survival—an organism with two or three neighbors will survive to the next generation. Possible generations 2 and 3 for the sample follow:

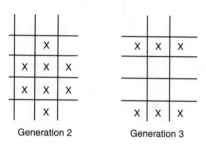

Generation 2   Generation 3

Take an initial configuration of organisms as input data. Display the original game array, calculate the next generation of organisms in a new array, copy the new array into the original game array, and repeat the cycle for as many generations as you wish. Hint: Assume that the borders of the game array are infertile regions where organisms can neither survive nor be born; you will not have to process the border squares.

4. The transpose of a matrix is formed by interchanging the matrix's rows and columns. Thus, the transpose of matrix

$$A = \begin{bmatrix} 2 & 4 \\ 6 & 8 \\ 10 & 12 \end{bmatrix} \quad \text{is} \quad A^t = \begin{bmatrix} 2 & 6 & 10 \\ 4 & 8 & 12 \end{bmatrix}$$

Write the transpose function modeled below, and use it in your solution to the following problem. Assume that the declared size of all matrices to be used is 10×10.

The organizers of an in-house software engineering conference for a small consulting company are trying to minimize scheduling conflicts by scheduling the most popular presentations at different times. First the planners survey the ten participants to determine which of the five presentations they want to attend. Then they construct a matrix A in which a 1 in entry ij means that participant i wants to attend presentation j.

Participant	Presentation				
	1	2	3	4	5
1	1	0	1	0	1
2	0	0	1	1	1
3	1	0	0	0	0
4	0	1	1	0	1
5	0	0	0	0	0
6	1	1	0	0	0

Presentation

Participant	1	2	3	4	5
7	0	0	1	0	1
8	0	1	0	1	0
9	1	0	1	0	1
10	0	0	0	1	0

Next, the planners calculate the transpose of A (A^t) and the matrix product A^tA. In the resulting matrix, entry ij is the number of participants wishing to attend both presentation i and presentation j.

$$A^tA = \begin{bmatrix} 4 & 1 & 2 & 0 & 2 \\ 1 & 3 & 1 & 1 & 1 \\ 2 & 1 & 5 & 1 & 5 \\ 0 & 1 & 1 & 3 & 1 \\ 2 & 1 & 5 & 1 & 5 \end{bmatrix}$$

Notice that A^tA is symmetric ($a_{ij} = a_{ji}$ for all i, j), so the entries below the main diagonal (entries ij where $i > j$) need not be calculated (see shaded region). If we supply zeros for the unnecessary entries, the resulting matrix is termed an *upper triangular matrix*. The entries on the main diagonal (a_{ii}) represent the total participants wanting to attend presentation i.

Write a program that inputs a matrix from a data file of participant preferences. The first line of this file should contain the matrix dimensions: For the preference matrix shown above, this line would be

```
10   5
```

Subsequent lines should be the rows of the matrix. After displaying the preference matrix A, calculate and display A^tA and output sentences indicating how many participants wish to attend each presentation. Finally, find the three largest numbers in the entries above the diagonal of A^tA, and display up to three pairs of presentations that the conference committee should avoid scheduling opposite one another. You will display fewer than three pairs if one (or more) of the three largest numbers is 1.

5. Figure 8.22 represents the flow of fluid in a system of pipes. The arrows indicate the direction of fluid flow, and the numbers just past each intersection indicate the portion of the fluid taking that path. For example, of the fluid reaching P_1, 40% flows to P_3 and 60% flows to P_2. Thus

$$x_1 = 0.4n_1$$
$$x_2 = 0.2(0.6n_1 + n_2) = 0.12n_1 + 0.2n_2$$
$$x_3 = 0.8(0.6n_1 + n_2) = 0.48n_1 + 0.8n_2$$

We can represent this system of linear equations as the matrix equation

Figure 8.22
Fluid Flow in System
of Pipes

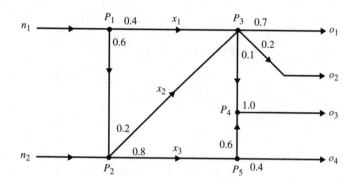

$$X = AN$$

where

$$X = \begin{bmatrix} x_1 \\ x_2 \\ x_3 \end{bmatrix} \qquad A = \begin{bmatrix} 0.40 & 0 \\ 0.12 & 0.2 \\ 0.48 & 0.8 \end{bmatrix} \qquad N = \begin{bmatrix} n_1 \\ n_2 \end{bmatrix}$$

Similarly,

$$O = BX$$

where

$$O = \begin{bmatrix} o_1 \\ o_2 \\ o_3 \\ o_4 \end{bmatrix} \qquad B = \begin{bmatrix} 0.7 & 0.7 & 0 \\ 0.2 & 0.2 & 0 \\ 0.1 & 0.1 & 0.6 \\ 0 & 0 & 0.4 \end{bmatrix}$$

Thus, the vector of outputs from the system is computed as the product of three matrices:

$$O = B(AN)$$

Write a program that takes from a data file a vector of input flows N and additional matrices $A, B, C, \ldots$, and computes the pipe system outputs by forming the matrix product $\ldots$ $C(B(AN))$.

6. Directed graphs (digraphs) are often used as models of communications networks. One of the most useful representations of an n-vertex digraph is an $n \times n$ adjacency matrix. Consider these three representations of the same digraph:

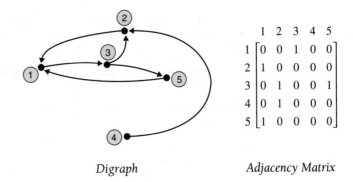

Digraph   *Adjacency Matrix*

Vertices: {1, 2, 3, 4, 5}

Edges: { (1,3), (2,1), (3,2), (3,5), (4,2), (5,1)}

Lists of Vertices and Edges

In the adjacency matrix, a 1 in entry *ij* means there is an edge from vertex *i* to vertex *j*. Write a program that converts an adjacency matrix to a list of edges and a list of edges to an adjacency matrix using the functions modeled below:

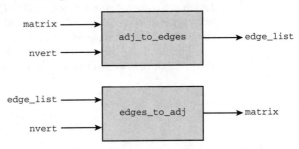

You may assume that the vertices of an *n*-vertex graph will be numbered from 1 to *n*, so a file representation of the edge list version of the digraph shown could be

```
5
1    3
2    1
3    2
3    5
4    2
5    1
```

Remember that your matrix subscripts will be one less than the corresponding vertex numbers. Allow for up to eight vertices—i.e., declare an adjacency matrix to be 8 × 8 and an edge-list matrix to be 64 × 2.

7. Write a program that will take a 4×4 *square matrix A* (same number of rows and columns) and a nonnegative integer p and will compute A^p, that is, *A raised to the power p*. A^p is defined as

$A^0 =$ *the identity matrix, I*   (all 0s except for 1s on the diagonal)
$A^p = A * A^{p-1}, p \geq 1$

8. Write a program that uses Gaussian elimination to solve each of the following systems of equations:

a. $x + 2y + z = 4$
     $2x + y - z = -1$
     $-x + y + z = 2$
b. $x - y + 2z = 3$
     $2x + 3y - 6z = 1$
     $4x + y - 2z = 7$
c. $3x - z = 7$
     $2x + y = 6$
     $3y - z = 7$

9. The *inverse of a square matrix A* is defined to be the matrix A_inv that satisfies

$$A * A\_inv = I \quad \text{(See the identity matrix in Project 7.)}$$

If A_inv exists, then A is said to be invertible. (If A is invertible, then A_inv is also invertible, and A is the inverse of A_inv.) The inverse of a matrix A can be computed using Gaussian elimination. This technique will also tell us if A is not invertible.

First let us describe with an example how to set up the data to find the inverse of a matrix A. Suppose we want to find the inverse of the following matrix:

$$A = \begin{bmatrix} 1 & 2 & 1 \\ 2 & 1 & -1 \\ -1 & 1 & 1 \end{bmatrix}$$

The problem solution is derived by setting up a work matrix W that has the original matrix A as its first three columns and the identity matrix as its last three columns:

$$A = \left[\begin{array}{ccc|ccc} 1 & 2 & 1 & 1 & 0 & 0 \\ 2 & 1 & -1 & 0 & 1 & 0 \\ -1 & 1 & 1 & 0 & 0 & 1 \end{array} \right]$$

We now apply Gaussian elimination to the three leftmost columns. However, we modify Gaussian elimination as presented in the text, so that the three leftmost columns become the identity matrix. In other words, it is not sufficient to get the three leftmost columns in scaled triangular form. Getting these columns in the correct form requires only a slight modification of the function gauss. When we eliminate coefficients in the pivot column, we do so both above and beneath the pivot.

The key to this method is that as we apply Gaussian elimination to the left half of W, we apply all row operations throughout the matrix W. When the left side of W is the identity matrix, the right side will contain the inverse of A. If Gaussian elimination fails because no nonzero pivot is found for a certain pivot element, then the original matrix A must be noninvertible.

Write a program that will take a square matrix and compute its inverse by this modification of Gaussian elimination.

CHAPTER 9

Structure
Types

QUICK-CHECK EXERCISES

1. What is the primary difference between a structure and an array? Which would you use to store the catalog description of a course? To store the names of students in the course?
2. How do you access a component of a structure type variable?

   Exercises 3–8 refer to the following type `student_t` and to variables `stu1` and `stu2`.

   ```
   typedef struct {
         char fst_name[20],
               last_name[20];
         int  score;
         char grade;
   } student_t;
   . . .
   student_t stu1, stu2;
   ```

3. Identify the following statements as possibly valid or definitely invalid. If invalid, explain why.

   a. `student_t stulist[30];`
   b. `printf("%s", stu1);`
   c. `printf("%d %c", stu1.score, stu1.grade);`
   d. `stu2 = stu1;`
   e. `if (stu2.score == stu1.score)`
         `printf("Equal");`
   f. `if (stu2 == stu1)`
         `printf("Equal structures");`
   g. `scan_student(&stu1);`
   h. `stu2.last_name = "Martin";`

4. Write a statement that displays the initials of `stu1` (with periods).
5. How many components does variable `stu2` have?
6. Write functions `scan_student` and `print_student` for type `student_t` variables.
7. Declare an array of 40 `student_t` structures, and write a code segment that displays on separate lines the names (*last name, first name*) of all the students in the list.
8. Identify the type of each of the following references:

   a. `stu1`
   b. `stu2.score`
   c. `stu2.fst_name[3]`
   d. `stu1.grade`

ANSWERS TO QUICK-CHECK EXERCISES

1. A structure can have components of different types, but an array's elements must all be of the same type. Use a structure for the catalog item and an array of strings for the list of student names.
2. Components of structures are accessed using the direct selection operator followed by a component name.
3. a. Valid
   b. Invalid: `printf` does not accept structured arguments.
   c. Valid
   d. Valid
   e. Valid
   f. Invalid: Equality operators cannot be used with structure types.
   g. Valid (assuming parameter type is `student_t *`)
   h. Invalid: cannot copy strings with = except in declaration (this case needs `strcpy`)
4. `printf("%c.%c.", stu1.fst_name[0],`
   `        stu1.last_name[0]);`
5. four
6.
```
int
scan_student(student_t *stup) /* output - student struc-
                                        ture to fill */
{
      int   status,
      char temp[4]; /* temporary storage for grade */
      status = scanf("%s%s%d %c",stu->fst_name,
                                 stu->last_name,
                                 &stu->score,
                                 &stu->grade);
      if (status == 4) {
          status = 1;
      } else if (status != EOF) {
          status = 0;
      }

      return (status);
}

void
print_student(student_t stu) /* input - student structure
                                      to display */
{
      printf("Student: %s, %s\n", stu.last_name,
          stu.fst_name);
      printf("   Score: %d      Grade: %c\n", stu.score,
          stu.grade);
}
```

```
7. student_t students[40];

   for  (i = 0;   i < 40;   ++i)
      printf("%s, %s\n", students[i].last_name,
             students[i].fst_name);
8. a. student_t
   b. int
   c. char
   d. char
```

REVIEW QUESTIONS

1. Define a structure type called subscriber_t that contains the components name, street_address, and monthly_bill (i.e., how much the subscriber owes).

2. Write a C program that scans data to fill the variable competition declared below and then displays the contents of the structure with suitable labels.

```
#define STR_LENGTH 20

typedef struct {
      char event[STR_LENGTH],
           entrant[STR_LENGTH],
           country[STR_LENGTH];
      int  place;
} olympic_t;
. . .
olympic_t competition;
```

3. How would you call a function scan_olympic passing competition as an output argument?

4. Identify and correct the errors in the following program:

```
typedef struct
      char   name[15],
             start_date[15],
      double hrs_worked,
summer_help_t;

/* prototype for function scan_sum_hlp goes here */

int
main(void)
{
      struct operator;

      scan_sum_hlp(operator);
      printf("Name: %s\nStarting date: %s\nHours worked:
             %.2f\n", operator);
```

```
    return(0);
}
```

5. Define a data structure to store the following student data: gpa, major, address (consisting of street address, city, state, zip), and class schedule (consisting of up to six class records, each of which has description, time, and days components). Define whatever data types are needed.

PROGRAMMING PROJECTS

1. Define a structure type vect_t to represent a vector as a magnitude r and a direction theta. Store component theta as an angle (in radians) in the range $[0, 2\pi)$. Define input and output functions scan_vector and print_vector. Define functions x_component and y_component that take a vect_t parameter and return the x component ($r \cos \theta$) and the y component ($r \sin \theta$), respectively. Also define a function add_vect that adds two type vect_t arguments returning a vect_t result. To do this calculation, first find the x and y components of the sum and then apply the Pythagorean theorem to determine the magnitude of the resultant vector. Check the signs of the x and y components to determine the quadrant of the resultant vector, and use the relation

$$\tan \theta = \frac{y_{sum}}{x_{sum}}$$

to find the direction of the vector. Since vect_t direction components should fall in the range $[0, 2\pi)$, you will need to adjust the angle computed by the arctangent function atan if the vector is not in quadrant I. The necessary adjustments follow:

Quadrant of Vector	Sign of y_{sum}/x_{sum}	Add to Angle
II	–	π
III	+	π
IV	–	2π

Test your functions by repeatedly scanning pairs of vectors and calculating and printing the sum of each pair until a zero vector is encountered.

2. Define a structure type auto_t to represent an automobile. Include components for the make and model (strings), the odometer reading, the manufacture and purchase dates (use another user-defined type called date_t), and the gas tank (use a user-defined type tank_t with components for tank capacity and current fuel level, giving both in gallons). Write I/O functions scan_date, scan_tank, scan_auto, print_date, print_tank, and print_auto, and also write a driver function that repeatedly fills and displays an auto structure variable until EOF is encountered in the input file.
   Here is a small data set to try:

```
Mercury Sable    99842 1 18 1989 5 30 1991 16    12.5
Mazda   Navajo   23961 2 20 1993 6 15 1993 19.3 16.7
```

3. Define a structure type `element_t` to represent one element from the periodic table of elements. Components should include the atomic number (an integer); the name, chemical symbol, and class (strings); a numeric field for the atomic weight; and a seven-element array of integers for the number of electrons in each shell. The following are the components of an `element_t` structure for sodium.

```
11   Sodium   Na   alkali_metal   22.9898   2 8 1 0 0 0 0
```

Define and test I/O functions `scan_element` and `print_element`.

4. A number expressed in scientific notation is represented by its mantissa (a fraction) and its exponent (an integer). Define a type `sci_not_t` that has separate components for these two parts. Define a function `scan_sci` that takes from the input source a string representing a positive number in scientific notation, and breaks it into components for storage in a `sci_not_t` structure. The mantissa of an input value (m) should satisfy this condition: $0.1 <= m < 1.0$. Also write functions to compute the sum, difference, product, and quotient of two `sci_not_t` values. All these functions should have a result type of `sci_not_t` and should ensure that the result's mantissa is in the prescribed range. Define a `print_sci` function as well. Then, create a driver program to test your functions. Your output should be of this form:

```
Values input:   0.25000e3   0.20000e1
Sum:   0.25200e3
Difference:   0.24800e3
Product:   0.50000e3
Quotient:   0.12500e3
```

5. Numeric addresses for computers on the international network Internet are composed of four parts, separated by periods, of the form

```
xx.yy.zz.mm
```

where xx, yy, zz, and mm are positive integers. Locally, computers are usually known by a nickname as well. You are designing a program to process a list of Internet addresses, identifying all pairs of computers from the same locality. Create a structure type called `address_t` with components for the four integers of an Internet address and a fifth component in which to store an associated nickname of 10 characters. Your program should read a list of up to 100 addresses and nicknames terminated by a sentinel address of all zeros and a sentinel nickname.

Sample Data
```
111.22.3.44      platte
555.66.7.88      wabash
111.22.5.66      green
0.0.0.0          none
```

The program should display a list of messages identifying each pair of computers from the same locality—that is, each pair of computers with matching values in the first two components of the address. In the messages, the computers should be identified by their nicknames.

Example Message

```
Machines platte and green are on the same local
network.
```

Follow the messages by a display of the full list of addresses and nicknames. Include in your program a scan_address function, a print_address function, and a local_address function. Function local_address should take two address structures as input parameters and return 1 (for true) if the addresses are on the same local network, and 0 (for false) otherwise.

6. Design and implement a structure type to model an ideal transformer. If you have a single iron core with wire 1 coiled around the core N_1 times and wire 2 wound around the core N_2 times, and if wire 1 is attached to a source of alternating current, then the voltage in wire 1 (the input voltage V_1) is related to the voltage in wire 2 (the output voltage V_2) as

$$\frac{V_1}{V_2} = \frac{N_1}{N_2}$$

and the relationship between the input current I_1 and the output current I_2 is

$$\frac{I_1}{I_2} = \frac{N_1}{N_2}$$

A variable of type transformer_t should store N_1, N_2, V_1, and I_1. Also define functions v_out and i_out to compute the output voltage and current of a transformer. In addition, define functions that set each of the transformer's components to produce a desired output voltage or current. For example, function set_n1_for_v2 should take a desired output voltage as an input parameter and a transformer as an input/output parameter and should change the component representing N_1 to produce the desired current. Also define set_v1_for_v2, set_n2_for_v2, and set_n2_for_i2. Include scan_transformer and print_transformer functions to facilitate I/O.

7. Create a structure type to represent a battery. A battery_t variable's components will include the voltage, how much energy the battery is capable of storing, and how much energy it is currently storing (in joules). Define functions for input and output of batteries. Create a function called power_device that (a) takes the current of an electrical device (amps) and the time the device is to be powered by the battery (seconds) as input parameters and (b) takes a battery as an input/output parameter. The function first determines whether the battery's energy reserve is adequate to power the device for the prescribed time. If so, the function updates the battery's energy reserve by subtracting the energy consumed and then returns the value true (1). Otherwise it returns the value false (0) and leaves the energy reserve unchanged. Also define a function named max_time that takes a battery and the current of an electrical device as input parameters and returns the number of seconds the battery can operate the device before it is fully discharged. This function does not change any of the battery's component values. Write a function recharge that sets to the maximum capacity the battery's component representing present energy reserve. Use the following equations in your design:

$$p = vi$$

$$w = pt$$

p = power in watts (W)

v = voltage in volts (V)

i = current in amps (A)

w = energy in joules (J)

t = time in seconds (s)

For this simulation, neglect any loss of energy in the transfer from battery to device.

Create a main function that declares and initializes a variable to model a 12-V automobile battery with a maximum energy storage of 5×10^6 J. Use the battery to power a 4-A light for 15 minutes, and then find out how long the battery's remaining energy could power an 8-A device. After recharging the battery, recalculate how long it could operate an 8-A device.

8. Using type `complex_t` from Section 9.4, develop a Gaussian elimination program to solve systems of linear equations with complex coefficients. Hint: Review Section 8.4.

9. Rewrite the common fraction program from Section 6.7 using a structure type to represent a fraction.

The following content was taken from

Problem Solving and Program Design in C, **Fifth Edition**
by Jeri R. Hanly and Elliot B. Koffman

CHAPTER 2

Overview of C

Quick-Check Exercises

1. What value is assigned to the type double variable x by the statement

   ```
   x = 25.0 * 3.0 / 2.5;
   ```

2. What value is assigned to x by the following statement, assuming x is 10.0?

   ```
   x = x - 20.0;
   ```

3. Show the exact form of the output line displayed when x is 3.456.

   ```
   printf("Three values of x are %4.1f*%5.2f*%.3f\n",
          x, x, x);
   ```

4. Show the exact form of the output line when n is 345.

    ```
    printf("Three values of n are %4d*%5d*%d\n",
             n, n, n);
    ```

5. What data types would you use to represent the following items: number of children at school, a letter grade on an exam, the average number of school days a child is absent each year?
6. In which step of the software development method are the problem inputs and outputs identified?
7. If function scanf is getting two numbers from the same line of input, what characters should be used to separate them?
8. How does the computer determine how many data values to get from the input device when a scanf operation is performed?
9. In an interactive program, how does the program user know how many data values to enter when the scanf function is called?
10. Does the compiler listing show syntax or run-time errors?

Answers to Quick-Check Exercises

1. `30.0`
2. `-10.0`
3. `Three values of x are ▉3.5*▉3.46*3.456` (▉ = 1 blank)
4. `Three values of n are ▉345*▉▉345*345`
5. `int, char, double`
6. analysis
7. blanks
8. It depends on the number of placeholders in the format string.
9. from reading the prompt
10. syntax errors

Review Questions

1. What type of information should be specified in the block comment at the very beginning of the program?
2. Which variables below are syntactically correct?

    ```
    income      two fold
    1time       c3po
    int         income#1
    Tom's       item
    ```

3. What is illegal about the following program fragment?

```
#include <stdio.h>
#define PI 3.14159
int
main(void)
{
      double c, r;

      scanf("%lf%lf", c, r);
      PI = c / (2 * r);
      . . .

}
```

4. Stylistically, which of the following identifiers would be good choices for names of constant macros?

```
gravity    G    MAX_SPEED    Sphere_Size
```

5. Write the data requirements, necessary formulas, and algorithm for Programming Project 9 in the next section.

6. The average pH of citrus fruits is 2.2, and this value has been stored in the variable `avg_citrus_pH`. Provide a statement to display this information in a readable way.

7. List three standard data types of C.

8. Convert the program statements below to take input data and echo it in batch mode.

```
printf("Enter two characters> ");
scanf("%c%c", &c1, &c2);
printf("Enter three integers separated by spaces> ");
scanf("%d%d%d", &n, &m, &p);
```

9. Write an algorithm that allows for the input of an integer value, doubles it, subtracts 10, and displays the result.

Programming Projects

1. Write a program that calculates mileage reimbursement for a salesperson at a rate of $.35 per mile. Your program should interact with the user in this manner:

```
MILEAGE REIMBURSEMENT CALCULATOR
Enter beginning odometer reading=> 13505.2
Enter ending odometer reading=> 13810.6
You traveled 305.4 miles.  At $.35 per mile,
your reimbursement is $106.89.
```

2. Write a program to assist in the design of a hydroelectric dam. Prompt the user for the height of the dam and for the number of cubic meters of water that are projected to flow from the top to the bottom of the dam each second. Predict how many megawatts ($1MW = 10^6W$) of power will be produced if 90% of the work done on the water by gravity is converted to electrical energy. Note that the mass of one cubic meter of water is 1000 kg. Use 9.80 meters/second^2 as the gravitational constant g. Be sure to use meaningful names for both the gravitational constant and the 90% efficiency constant. For one run, use a height of 170 m and flow of 1.30×10^3 m^3/s. The relevant formula (w = work, m=mass, g=gravity, h = height) is: $w = mgh$

3. Write a program that estimates the temperature in a freezer (in °C) given the elapsed time (hours) since a power failure. Assume this temperature (T) is given by

$$T = \frac{4t^2}{t + 2} - 20$$

where t is the time since the power failure. Your program should prompt the user to enter how long it has been since the start of the power failure in whole hours and minutes. Note that you will need to convert the elapsed time into hours. For example, if the user entered 2 30 (2 hours 30 minutes), you would need to convert this to 2.5 hours.

4. Write a program to convert a temperature in degrees Fahrenheit to degrees Celsius.

DATA REQUIREMENTS

Problem Input

`int fahrenheit /* temperature in degrees Fahrenheit     */`

Problem Output

`double celsius /* temperature in degrees Celsius          */`

Relevant Formula

celsius = 5/9 (*fahrenheit* − 32)

5. Write a program to take two numbers as input data and display their sum, their difference, their product, and their quotient.

DATA REQUIREMENTS

Problem Inputs

```
double x, y        /* two items */
```

Problem Outputs

```
double sum          /* sum of x and y            */
double difference /* difference of x and y     */
double product      /* product of x and y        */
double quotient     /* quotient of x divided by y */
```

6. Write a program that predicts the score needed on a final exam to achieve a desired grade in a course. The program should interact with the user as follows:

```
Enter desired grade> B
Enter minimum average required> 79.5
Enter current average in course> 74.6
Enter how much the final counts
as a percentage of the course grade> 25

You need a score of 94.20 on the final to get a B.
```

In the example shown, the final counts 25 percent of the course grade.

7. Write a program that calculates how many Btus of heat are delivered to a house given the number of gallons of oil burned and the efficiency of the house's oil furnace. Assume that a barrel of oil (42 gallons) has an energy equivalent of 5,800,000 Btu. (*Note:* This number is too large to represent as an int on some personal computers.) For one test use an efficiency of 65 percent and 100 gallons of oil.

8. Metro City Planners proposes that a community conserve its water supply by replacing all the community's toilets with low-flush models that use only 2 liters per flush. Assume that there is about 1 toilet for every 3 persons, that existing toilets use an average of 15 liters per flush, that a toilet is flushed on average 14 times per day, and that the cost to install each new toilet is $150. Write a program that would estimate the magnitude (liters/day) and cost of the water saved based on the community's population.

9. Write a program that takes the length and width of a rectangular yard and the length and width of a rectangular house situated in the yard. Your program should compute the time required to cut the grass at the rate of two square feet a second.

10. Write a program that takes as input the numerators and denominators of two fractions. Your program should display the numerator and denominator of the fraction that represents the product of the two fractions. Also, display the percent equivalent of the resulting product.

11. Redo Project 10; this time compute the sum of the two fractions.

12. The Pythagorean theorem states that the sum of the squares of the sides of a right triangle is equal to the square of the hypotenuse. For example, if two sides of a right triangle have lengths of 3 and 4, then the hypotenuse must have a length of 5. Together the integers 3, 4, and 5 form a *Pythagorean triple*. There are an infinite number of such triples. Given two positive integers, m and n, where $m > n$, a Pythagorean triple can be generated by the following formulas:

$$side1 = m^2 - n^2$$

$$side2 = 2mn$$

$$hypotenuse = m^2 + n^2$$

The triple ($side1$ = 3, $side2$ = 4, $hypotenuse$ = 5) is generated by this formula when m = 2 and n = 1. Write a program that takes values for m and n as input and displays the values of the Pythagorean triple generated by the formulas above.

13. Write a program that calculates the acceleration (m/s²) of a jet fighter launched from an aircraft-carrier catapult, given the jet's takeoff speed in km/hr and the distance (meters) over which the catapult accelerates the jet from rest to takeoff. Assume constant acceleration. Also calculate the time (seconds) for the fighter to be accelerated to takeoff speed. When you prompt the user, be sure to indicate the units for each input. For one run, use a takeoff speed of 278 km/hr and a distance of 94 meters. Relevant formulas (v = velocity, a = acceleration, t = time, s = distance)

$$v = at$$

$$s = \frac{1}{2} at^2$$

Top-Down Design with Functions

Quick-Check Exercises

1. Developing a program from its documentation means that every statement in the program has a comment. True or false?
2. The principle of code reuse states that every function in your program must be used more than once. True or false?
3. Write this equation as a C statement using functions exp, log, and pow:

$$y = (e^{n \ln b})^2$$

4. What is the purpose of a function argument?
5. Each function is executed in the order in which it is defined in the source file. True or false?
6. How is a function in a C program executed?
7. What is a formal parameter?
8. Explain how a structure chart differs from an algorithm.
9. What does the following function do?

```
void
nonsense(void)
{
```

```
        printf("*****\n");
        printf("*   *\n");
        printf("*****\n");
    }
```

10. What does the following main function do?

```
int
main(void)
{
        nonsense();
        nonsense();
        nonsense();

        return (0);
}
```

11. If an actual argument of -35.7 is passed to a type int formal parameter, what will happen? If an actual argument of 17 is passed to a type double formal parameter, what will happen?

Answers to Quick-Check Exercises

1. False
2. False
3. `y = pow(exp(n * log(b)), 2);`
4. A function argument is used to pass information into a function.
5. False
6. It is called into execution by a function call—that is, the function name followed by its arguments in parentheses.
7. A formal parameter is used in a function definition to represent a corresponding actual argument.
8. A structure chart shows the subordinate relationships between subproblems; an algorithm lists the sequence in which subproblem solutions are carried out.
9. It displays a rectangle of asterisks.
10. It displays three rectangles of asterisks on top of each other.
11. The formal parameter's value will be -35. The formal parameter's value will be 17.0.

Review Questions

1. Define top-down design and structure charts.
2. What is a function prototype?
3. When is a function executed, and where should a function prototype and function definition appear in a source program?
4. What are three advantages of using functions?
5. Is the use of functions a more efficient use of the programmer's time or the computer's time? Explain your answer.
6. Write a program that prompts the user for the two legs of a right triangle and makes use of the `pow` and `sqrt` functions and the Pythagorean theorem to compute the length of the hypotenuse.
7. Write a program that draws a rectangle made of a double border of asterisks. Use two functions: `draw_sides` and `draw_line`.
8. Draw a structure chart for the program described in Review Question 7.
9. Write the prototype for a function called `script` that has three input parameters. The first parameter will be the number of spaces to display at the beginning of a line. The second parameter will be the character to display after the spaces, and the third parameter will be the number of times to display the second parameter on the same line.

Programming Projects

1. You have saved $500 to use as a down payment on a car. Before beginning your car shopping, you decide to write a program to help you figure out what your monthly payment will be, given the car's purchase price, the monthly interest rate, and the time period over which you will pay back the loan. The formula for calculating your payment is

$$payment = \frac{iP}{1 - (1 + i)^{-n}}$$

where

P = principal (the amount you borrow)
i = monthly interest rate ($\frac{1}{12}$ of the annual rate)
n = total number of payments

Your program should prompt the user for the purchase price, the down payment, the annual interest rate and the total number of payments (usually 36, 48, or 60). It should then display the amount borrowed and the monthly payment including a dollar sign and two decimal places.

2. Write two functions, one that displays a triangle and one that displays a rectangle. Use these functions to write a complete C program from the following outline:

```
int
main(void)
{
     /* Draw triangle. */
     /* Draw rectangle. */
     /* Display 2 blank lines. */
     /* Draw triangle. */
     /* Draw rectangle. */

}
```

3. Add the functions from Fig. 3.14 to the ones for Programming Project 2. Use these functions in a program that draws a rocket ship (triangle over rectangles over intersecting lines), a male stick figure (circle over rectangle over intersecting lines), and a female stick figure standing on the head of a male stick figure. Write function skip_5_lines and call it to place five blank lines between drawings.

4. Write a computer program that computes the duration of a projectile's flight and its height above the ground when it reaches the target. As part of your solution, write and call a function that displays instructions to the program user.

Problem Constant

`G 32.17 /* gravitational constant      */`

Problem Inputs

```
double theta /* input - angle (radians) of elevation    */
double distance /* input - distance (ft) to target        */
double velocity /* input - projectile velocity (ft/sec)   */
```

Problem Outputs

```
double time    /* output - time (sec) of flight          */
double height /* output - height at impact              */
```

Relevant Formulas

$$time = \frac{distance}{velocity \times \cos{(theta)}}$$

$$height = velocity \times \sin{(theta)} \times time - \frac{g \times time^2}{2}$$

Try your program on these data sets.

Inputs	Data Set 1	Data Set 2
angle of elevation	0.3 radian	0.71 radian
velocity	800 ft/sec	1,600 ft/sec
distance to target	11,000 ft	78,670 ft

5. Write a program that takes a positive number with a fractional part and rounds it to two decimal places. For example, 32.4851 would round to 32.49, and 32.4431 would round to 32.44. (*Hint:* See "Rounding a number" in table 2.9 and function `scale` in Fig. 3.23.)

6. Four track stars have entered the mile race at the Penn Relays. Write a program that scans in the race time in minutes (`minutes`) and seconds (`seconds`) for a runner and computes and displays the speed in feet per second (`fps`) and in meters per second (`mps`). (*Hints:* There are 5,280 feet in one mile, and one kilometer equals 3,282 feet.) Write and call a function that displays instructions to the program user. Run the program for each star's data.

Minutes	Seconds
3	52.83
3	59.83
4	00.03
4	16.22

7. In shopping for a new house, you must consider several factors. In this problem the initial cost of the house, the estimated annual fuel costs, and the annual tax rate are available. Write a program that will determine the total cost of a house after a five-year period and run the program for each of the following sets of data.

Initial House Cost	Annual Fuel Cost	Tax Rate
67,000	2,300	0.025
62,000	2,500	0.025
75,000	1,850	0.020

To calculate the house cost, add the initial cost to the fuel cost for five years, then add the taxes for five years. Taxes for one year are computed by multiplying the tax rate by the initial cost. Write and call a function that displays instructions to the program user.

8. A cyclist coasting on a level road slows from a speed of 10 mi/hr to 2.5 mi/hr in one minute. Write a computer program that calculates the cyclist's constant rate of acceleration and determines how long the cyclist will take to come to rest, given an initial speed of 10 mi/hr. (*Hint:* Use the equation

$$a = \frac{v_f - v_i}{t}$$

where a is acceleration, t is time interval, v_i is initial velocity, and v_f is final velocity.) Write and call a function that displays instructions to the program user and a function that computes a, given t, v_f, and v_i.

9. A manufacturer wishes to determine the cost of producing an open-top cylindrical container. The surface area of the container is the sum of the area of the circular base plus the area of the outside (the circumference of the base times the height of the container). Write a program to take the radius of the base, the height of the container, the cost per square centimeter of the material (cost), and the number of containers to be produced (quantity). Calculate the cost of each container and the total cost of producing all the containers. Write and call a function that displays instructions to the user and a function that computes surface area.

10. Write a program to take a depth (in kilometers) inside the earth as input data; compute and display the temperature at this depth in degrees Celsius and degrees Fahrenheit. The relevant formulas are

$$Celsius = 10\,(depth) + 20 \qquad \text{(Celsius temperature at depth in km)}$$
$$Fahrenheit = 1.8\,(Celsius) + 32$$

Include two functions in your program. Function celsius_at_depth should compute and return the Celsius temperature at a depth measured in kilometers. Function fahrenheit should convert a Celsius temperature to Fahrenheit.

11. The ratio between successive speeds of a six-speed gearbox (assuming that the gears are evenly spaced to allow for whole teeth) is

$$\sqrt[3]{M/m}$$

where M is the maximum speed in revolutions per minute and m is the minimum speed. Write a function speeds_ratio that calculates this ratio for any maximum and minimum speeds. Write a main function that prompts for maximum and minimum speeds (rpm), calls speeds_ratio to calculate the ratio, and displays the results in a sentence of the form

The ratio between successive speeds of a six-speed gearbox with maximum speed _____ rpm and minimum speed _____ rpm is _____.

12. Write a program that calculates the speed of sound (a) in air of a given temperature T (°F). Use the formula:

$$a = 1086\,ft\,\sqrt{\frac{5T + 297}{247}}$$

Be sure your program does not lose the fractional part of the quotient in the formula shown. As part of your solution, write and call a function that displays instructions to the program user.

CHAPTER 4

Selection Structures:
if and switch
Statements

Quick-Check Exercises

1. An `if` statement implements _____ execution.
2. What is a compound statement?
3. A `switch` statement is often used instead of _____ .
4. What can be the values of an expression with a relational operator?
5. The relational operator `<=` means _____ .
6. A hand trace is used to verify that a(n) _____ is correct.
7. List the three types of control structures.
8. Correct the syntax errors.

```
if x > 25.0 {
        y = x
else
        y = z;
}
```

9. What value is assigned to `fee` by the `if` statement when `speed` is 75?

```
if (speed > 35)
        fee = 20.0;
else if (speed > 50)
        fee = 40.00;
else if (speed > 75)
        fee = 60.00;
```

10. Answer Exercise 9 for the `if` statement that follows. Which `if` statement seems reasonable?

```
if (speed > 75)
        fee = 60.0;
else if (speed > 50)
        fee = 40.00;
else if (speed > 35)
        fee = 20.00;
```

11. What output line(s) are displayed by the statements that follow when `grade` is `'I'`? When `grade` is `'B'`? When `grade` is `'b'`?

```
switch (grade) {
case 'A':
        points = 4;
        break;

case 'B':
        points = 3;
        break;

case 'C':
        points = 2;
        break;

case 'D':
        points = 1;
        break;
case 'E':
case 'I':
case 'W':
        points = 0;
}
```

```
if (points > 0)
      printf("Passed, points earned = %d\n", points);
else
      printf("Failed, no points earned\n");
```

12. Explain the difference between the statements on the left and the statements on the right. For each group of statements, give the final value of x if the initial value of x is 1.

```
if (x >= 0)              if (x >= 0)
      x = x + 1;               x = x + 1;
else if (x >= 1)         if (x >= 1)
      x = x + 2;               x = x + 2;
```

13. a. Evaluate the expression

    1 && (30 % 10 >= 0) && (30 % 10 <= 3)

  b. Is either set of parentheses required?
  c. Write the complement of the expression two ways. First, add one operator and one set of parentheses. For the second version, use DeMorgan's theorem.

Answers to Quick-Check Exercises

1. conditional
2. one or more statements surrounded by braces
3. nested `if` statements or a multiple-alternative `if` statement
4. 0 and 1
5. less than or equal to
6. algorithm
7. sequence, selection, repetition
8. Parenthesize condition, remove braces (or add them around `else:` `} else {`), and add a semicolon to the first assignment statement.
9. 20.00 (first condition is met)
10. 40.00, the one in 10

11. when grade is `'I'`:
    Failed, no points earned
    when grade is `'B'`:
    Passed, points earned = 3
    when grade is `'b'`:

    The `switch` statement is skipped so the output printed depends on the previous value of `points` (which may be garbage).

12. A nested `if` statement is on the left; a sequence of `if` statements is on the right. On the left `x` becomes 2; on the right `x` becomes 4.

13. a. 1
    b. no
    c. `!(1   &&   (30 % 10 >= 0)   &&   (30 % 10 <= 3))`
       `0  ||   (30 % 10 < 0)   ||   (30 % 10 > 3)`

Review Questions

1. Making a decision between two alternative courses of action is usually implemented with a(n) _____ statement in C.

2. Trace the following program fragment; indicate which function will be called if a data value of `27.34` is entered.

   ```
   printf("Enter a temperature> ");
   scanf("%lf", &temp);
   if (temp > 32.0)
         not_freezing();
   else
         ice_forming();
   ```

3. Write a multiple-alternative `if` statement to display a message indicating the educational level of a student based on the student's number of years of schooling (0, none; 1–5, elementary school; 6–8, middle school; 9–12, high school; more than 12, college). Print a message to indicate bad data as well.

4. Write a `switch` statement to select an operation based on the value of `inventory`. Increment `total_paper` by `paper_order` if `inventory` is `'B'` or `'C'`; increment `total_ribbon` by `ribbon_order` if `inventory` is `'E'`, `'F'`, or `'D'`; increment `total_label` by `label_order` if `inventory` is `'A'` or `'X'`. Do nothing if `inventory` is `'M'`. Display an error message if the value of `inventory` is not one of these eight letters.

5. Write an `if` statement that displays an acceptance message for an astronaut candidate if the person's weight is between the values of `opt_min` and

FIGURE 4.13 Flow Diagram for Review Question 6

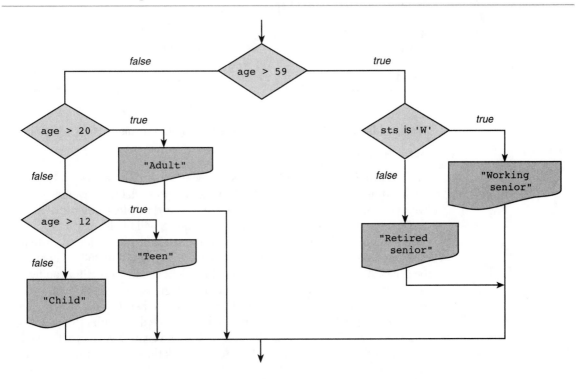

opt_max inclusive, the person's age is between `age_min` and `age_max` inclusive, and the person is a nonsmoker (`smoker` is false).

6. Implement the flow diagram in Fig. 4.13 using a nested `if` structure.

Programming Projects

1. Keith's Sheet Music needs a program to implement its music teacher's discount policy. The program is to prompt the user to enter the purchase total and to indicate whether the purchaser is a teacher. The store plans to give each customer a printed receipt, so your program is to create a nicely formatted file called receipt.txt. Music teachers receive a 10% discount on their sheet music purchases unless the purchase total is $100 or higher. In that case, the discount is 12%. The discount calculation occurs before addition of the 5% sales tax. Here are two sample output files—one for a teacher and one for a nonteacher.

```
Total purchases                        $122.00
Teacher's discount (12%)                 14.64
Discounted total                        107.36
Sales tax (5%)                            5.37
Total                                  $112.73

Total purchases                        $ 24.90
Sales tax (5%)                            1.25
Total                                  $ 26.15
```

Note: to display a % sign, place two % signs in the format string:

```
printf("%d%%", SALES_TAX);
```

2. Write a program that displays a message consisting of three block letters; each letter is either an x or an o. The program user's data determines whether a particular letter will be an x or o. For example, if the user enters the three letters xox, the block letters x, o, and x will be displayed.

3. While spending the summer as a surveyor's assistant, you decide to write a program that transforms compass headings in degrees (0 to 360) to compass bearings. A compass bearing consists of three items: the direction you face (north or south), an angle between 0 and 90 degrees, and the direction you turn before walking (east or west). For example, to get the bearing for a compass heading of 110.0 degrees, you would first face due south (180 degrees) and then turn 70.0 degrees east (180.0 − 70.0 is 110.0). Therefore, the bearing is South 70.0 degrees East. Be sure to check the input for invalid compass headings.

4. Write a program that reports the contents of a compressed-gas cylinder based on the first letter of the cylinder's color. The program input is a character representing the observed color of the cylinder: 'Y' or 'y' for yellow, 'O' or 'o' for orange, and so on. Cylinder colors and associated contents are as follows:

    orange   ammonia
    brown   carbon monoxide
    yellow   hydrogen
    green   oxygen

    Your program should respond to input of a letter other than the first letters of the given colors with the message, Contents unknown.

5. The National Earthquake Information Center has asked you to write a program implementing the following decision table to characterize an earthquake based on its Richter scale number.

Richter Scale Number (n)	Characterization
$n < 5.0$	Little or no damage
$5.0 \leq n < 5.5$	Some damage
$5.5 \leq n < 6.5$	Serious damage: walls may crack or fall
$6.5 \leq n < 7.5$	Disaster: houses and buildings may collapse
higher	Catastrophe: most buildings destroyed

Could you handle this problem with a `switch` statement? If so, use a `switch` statement; if not, explain why.

6. Write a program that takes the x–y coordinates of a point in the Cartesian plane and prints a message telling either an axis on which the point lies or the quadrant in which it is found.

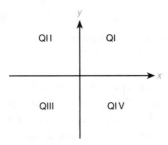

Sample lines of output:

```
(-1.0, -2.5) is in quadrant III
(0.0, 4.8) is on the y axis
```

7. Write a program that determines the day number (1 to 366) in a year for a date that is provided as input data. As an example, January 1, 1994, is day 1. December 31, 1993, is day 365. December 31, 1996, is day 366, since 1996 is a leap year. A year is a leap year if it is divisible by four, except that any year divisible by 100 is a leap year only if it is divisible by 400. Your program should accept the month, day, and year as integers. Include a function `leap` that returns 1 if called with a leap year, 0 otherwise.

8. Write a program that interacts with the user like this:

```
(1) Carbon monoxide
(2) Hydrocarbons
(3) Nitrogen oxides
(4) Nonmethane hydrocarbons
Enter pollutant number>> 2
Enter number of grams emitted per mile>> 0.35
Enter odometer reading>> 40112
Emissions exceed permitted level of 0.31 grams/mile.
```

Use the table of emissions limits below to determine the appropriate message.[1]

	First 50,000 Miles	Second 50,000 Miles
carbon monoxide	3.4 grams/mile	4.2 grams/mile
hydrocarbons	0.31 grams/mile	0.39 grams/mile
nitrogen oxides	0.4 grams/mile	0.5 grams/mile
nonmethane hydrocarbons	0.25 grams/mile	0.31 grams/mile

9. Write a program that will calculate and print bills for the city power company. The rates vary depending on whether the use is residential, commercial, or industrial. A code of R means residential use, a code of C means commercial use, and a code of I means industrial use. Any other code should be treated as an error.

    The rates are computed as follows:

    R: $6.00 plus $0.052 per kwh used
    C: $60.00 for the first 1000 kwh and $0.045 for each additional kwh
    I: Rate varies depending on time of usage:

    Peak hours: $76.00 for first 1000 kwh
        and $0.065 for each additional kwh
    Off-peak hours: $40.00 for first 1000 kwh
        and $0.028 for each additional kwh.

    Your program should prompt the user to enter an integer account number, the use code (type char), and the necessary consumption figures in whole numbers of kilowatt-hours. Your program should display the amount due from the user.

[1]Adapted from Joseph Priest, *Energy: Principles, Problems, Alternatives* (Reading, MA.: Addison-Wesley, 1991), p. 164.

10. Write a program to control a bread machine. Allow the user to input the type of bread as W for White and S for Sweet. Ask the user if the loaf size is double and if the baking is manual. The following table details the time chart for the machine for each bread type. Display a statement for each step. If the loaf size is double, increase the baking time by 50 percent. If baking is manual, stop after the loaf-shaping cycle and instruct the user to remove the dough for manual baking. Use functions to display instructions to the user and to compute the baking time.

BREAD TIME CHART

Operation	White Bread	Sweet Bread
Primary kneading	15 mins	20 mins
Primary rising	60 mins	60 mins
Secondary kneading	18 mins	33 mins
Secondary rising	20 mins	30 mins
Loaf shaping	2 seconds	2 seconds
Final rising	75 mins	75 mins
Baking	45 mins	35 mins
Cooling	30 mins	30 mins

11. The table below shows the normal boiling points of several substances. Write a program that prompts the user for the observed boiling point of a substance in °C and identifies the substance if the observed boiling point is within 5% of the expected boiling point. If the data input is more than 5% higher or lower than any of the boiling points in the table, the program should output the message Substance unknown.

Substance	Normal boiling point (°C)
Water	100
Mercury	357
Copper	1187
Silver	2193
Gold	2660

Your program should define and call a function `within_x_percent` that takes as parameters a reference value `ref`, a data value `data`, and a percentage value `x` and returns 1 meaning true if `data` is within x % of `ref`—that is, `(ref - x% * ref) ≤ data ≤ (ref + x % * ref)`. Otherwise within_x_percent would return zero, meaning false. For example, the call `within_x_percent(357, 323, 10)` would return true, since 10% of 357 is 35.7, and 323 falls between 321.3 and 392.7.

CHAPTER 5

Repetition and Loop Statements

Quick-Check Exercises

1. A loop that continues to process input data until a special value is entered is called a _____ -controlled loop.
2. Some `for` loops cannot be rewritten in C using a `while` loop. True or false?
3. It is an error if the body of a `for` loop never executes. True or false?
4. In an endfile-controlled `while` loop, the initialization and update expressions typically include calls to the function _____.
5. In a typical counter-controlled loop, the number of loop repetitions may not be known until the loop is executing. True or false?
6. During execution of the following program segment, how many lines of asterisks are displayed?

```
for  (i = 0;  i < 10;  ++i)
    for  (j = 0;  j < 5;  ++j)
        printf("**********\n");
```

7. During execution of the following program segment:

   a. How many times does the first call to `printf` execute?
   b. How many times does the second call to `printf` execute?
   c. What is the last value displayed?

```
for  (i = 0;  i < 7;  ++i) {
    for  (j = 0;  j < i;  ++j)
        printf("%4d", i * j);
    printf("\n");
}
```

8. If the value of n is 4 and m is 5, is the value of the following expression 21?

```
++(n * m)
```

Explain your answer.

9. What are the values of n, m, and p after execution of this three-statement fragment?

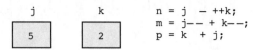

10. What are the values of x, y, and z after execution of this three-statement fragment?

11. What does the following code segment display? Try each of these inputs: 345, 82, 6. Then, describe the action of the code.

```
printf("\nEnter a positive integer> ");
scanf("%d", &num);
do {
     printf("%d  ", num % 10);
     num /= 10;
} while (num > 0);
printf("\n");
```

Answers to Quick-Check Exercises

1. sentinel
2. false
3. false
4. `fscanf`
5. false
6. `50`
7. a. `0 + 1 + 2 + 3 + 4 + 5 + 6 = 21`
   b. `7`
   c. `30`

8. No. The expression is illegal. The increment operator cannot be applied to an expression such as (n * m).
9. n=2, m=8, p=6
10. x=21, y=1, z=23
11.
```
Enter a positive integer> 345
5   4   3
Enter a positive integer> 82
2   8
Enter a positive integer> 6
6
```

The code displays the digits of an integer in reverse order and separated by spaces.

Review Questions

1. In what ways are the initialization, repetition test, and update steps alike for a sentinel-controlled loop and an endfile-controlled loop? How are they different?
2. Write a program that computes and displays the sum of a collection of Celsius temperatures entered at the terminal until a sentinel value of -275 is entered.
3. Hand trace the program that follows given the following data:

```
4 2 8 4   1 4 2 1   9 3 3 1   -22 10 8 2   3 3 4 5
#include <stdio.h>
#define SPECIAL_SLOPE   0.0

int
main(void)
{
      double slope, y2, y1, x2, x1;

      printf("Enter 4 numbers separated by spaces.");
      printf("\nThe last two numbers cannot be the ");
      printf("same, but\nthe program terminates if ");
      printf("the first two are.\n");
      printf("\nEnter four numbers> ");
      scanf("%lf%lf%lf%lf", &y2, &y1, &x2, &x1);

      for (slope = (y2 - y1) / (x2 - x1);
           slope != SPECIAL_SLOPE;
           slope = (y2 - y1) / (x2 - x1)) {
```

```
            printf("Slope is %5.2f.\n", slope);
            printf("\nEnter four more numbers> ");
            scanf("%lf%lf%lf%lf", &y2, &y1, &x2, &x1);
      }

            return (0);
}
```

4. Rewrite the program in Review Question 3 so that it uses a `while` loop.
5. Rewrite the program segment that follows, using a `for` loop:

```
count = 0;
i = 0;
while (i < n) {
    scanf("%d", &x);
    if (x == i)
            ++count;
    ++i;
}
```

6. Rewrite this `for` loop heading, omitting any invalid semicolons.

```
for (i = n;
     i < max;
     ++i; );
```

7. Write a `do-while` loop that repeatedly prompts for and takes input until a value in the range 0 through 15 inclusive is input. Include code that prevents the loop from cycling indefinitely on input of a wrong data type.

Programming Projects

1. Write a program to create an output file containing a customized loan amortization table. Your program will prompt the user to enter the amount borrowed (the *principal*), the annual interest rate, and the number of payments (*n*). To calculate the monthly payment, it will use the formula from Programming Project 1 in Chapter 3. This payment must be rounded to the nearest cent. After the payment has been rounded to the nearest cent, the program will write to the output file *n* lines showing how the debt is paid off. Each month part of the payment is the monthly interest on the principal balance, and the rest is applied to the principal. Because the payment and each month's interest are rounded, the final payment will be a bit different and must be calculated as the sum of the final interest payment and the final principal balance. Here is a sample table for a $1000 loan borrowed at a 9% annual interest rate and paid back over six months.

Payment Balance	Interest	Principal	Principal
Principal	$1000.00	Payment	$171.07
Annual interest	9.0%	Term	6 months

Payment Balance	Interest	Principal	Principal
1	7.50	163.57	836.43
2	6.27	164.80	671.63
3	5.04	166.03	505.60
4	3.79	167.28	338.32
5	2.54	168.53	169.79
6	1.27	169.79	0.00
Final payment	$171.06		

2. a. Write a program that will find the smallest, largest, and average values in a collection of *N* numbers. Get the value of *N* before scanning each value in the collection of *N* numbers.
    b. Modify your program to compute and display both the range of values in the data collection and the standard deviation of the data collection. To compute the standard deviation, accumulate the sum of the squares of the data values (sum_squares) in the main loop. After loop exit, use the formula

$$standard\ deviation = \sqrt{\frac{\texttt{sum\_squares}}{N} - average^2}$$

3. The greatest common divisor (gcd) of two integers is the product of the integers' common factors. Write a program that inputs two numbers and implements the following approach to finding their gcd. We will use the numbers −252 and 735. Working with the numbers' absolute values, we find the remainder of one divided by the other.

$$\begin{array}{r} 0 \\ 735\overline{)252} \\ \underline{0} \\ 252 \end{array}$$

Now we calculate the remainder of the old divisor divided by the remainder found.

```
       2
252 ) 735
      504
      ---
      231
```

We repeat this process until the remainder is zero.

```
       1            11
231 ) 252      21 ) 231
      231            21
      ---           ---
       21            21
                     21
                    ---
                      0
```

The last divisor (21) is the gcd.

4. The Environmental Awareness Club of BigCorp International is proposing that the company subsidize at $.08 per passenger km the commuting costs of employees who form carpools that meet a prescribed minimum passenger efficiency. Passenger efficiency *P* (in passenger-kilometers per liter) is defined as

$$P = \frac{ns}{l}$$

where n is the number of passengers, s is the distance traveled in km, and l is the number of liters of gasoline used.

Write a program that prompts the user for a minimum passenger efficiency and then processes an input file of data on existing carpools (`carpool.txt`), creating an ouput file `effic.txt` containing a table of all carpools that meet the passenger efficiency minimum. The input file represents each carpool as a data line containing three numbers: the number of people in the carpool, the total commuting distance per five-day week, and the number of liters of gasoline consumed in a week of commuting. The data file ends with a line of zeros. Write your results with this format:

```
           CARPOOLS MEETING MINIMUM PASSENGER EFFICIENCY OF 25 PASSENGER KM / L
Passengers        Weekly Commute        Gasoline              Efficiency          Weekly
                  (km)                  Consumption(L)        (pass km / L)       Subsidy($)
4                 75                    11.0                  27.3                24.00
2                 60                    4.5                   26.7                19.60
...
```

5. Let n be a positive integer consisting of up to 10 digits, $d_{10}, d_9, \ldots, d_1$. Write a program to list in one column each of the digits in the number n. The right-most digit, d_1, should be listed at the top of the column. *Hint:* If n is 3,704, what is the value of the digit when computed by using

    ```
    digit = n % 10;
    ```

    Test your program for values of n equal to 6; 3,704; and 170,498.

6. a. Write a program to process a collection of daily high temperatures. Your program should count and print the number of hot days (high temperature 85 or higher), the number of pleasant days (high temperature 60–84), and the number of cold days (high temperatures less than 60). It should also display the category of each temperature. Test your program on the following data:

    ```
    55  62  68  74  59  45  41  58  60  67  65  78  82  88  91
    92  90  93  87  80  78  79  72  68  61  59
    ```

    b. Modify your program to display the average temperature (a real number) at the end of the run.

7. Write a program to process weekly employee time cards for all employees of an organization. Each employee will have three data items: an identification number, the hourly wage rate, and the number of hours worked during a given week. Each employee is to be paid time and a half for all hours worked over 40. A tax amount of 3.625 percent of gross salary will be deducted. The program output should show the employee's number and net pay. Display the total payroll and the average amount paid at the end of the run.

8. Suppose you own a beer distributorship that sells Piels (ID number 1), Coors (ID number 2), Bud (ID number 3), and Iron City (ID number 4) by the case. Write a program to

    a. Get the case inventory for each brand for the start of the week.
    b. Process all weekly sales and purchase records for each brand.
    c. Display out the final inventory.

    Each transaction will consist of two data items. The first item will be the brand ID number (an integer). The second will be the amount purchased (a positive integer value) or the amount sold (a negative integer value). For now you may assume that you always have sufficient foresight to prevent depletion of your inventory for any brand. (*Hint:* Your data entry should begin with four values representing the case inventory, followed by the transaction values.)

9. The pressure of a gas changes as the volume and temperature of the gas vary. Write a program that uses the Van der Waals equation of state for a gas,

$$\left(P + \frac{an^2}{V^2}\right)(V - bn) = nRT$$

to create a file that displays in tabular form the relationship between the pressure and the volume of n moles of carbon dioxide at a constant absolute temperature (T). P is the pressure in atmospheres, and V is the volume in liters. The Van der Waals constants for carbon dioxide are a = 3.592 L^2 · atm/mol^2 and b = 0.0427 L/mol. Use 0.08206 L · atm/mol · K for the gas constant R. Inputs to the program include n, the Kelvin temperature, the initial and final volumes in milliliters, and the volume increment between lines of the table. Your program will output a table that varies the volume of the gas from the initial to the final volume in steps prescribed by the volume increment. Here is a sample run:

```
Please enter at the prompts the number of moles of carbon
dioxide, the absolute temperature, the initial volume in
milliliters, the final volume, and the increment volume
between lines of the table.

Quantity of carbon dioxide (moles)> 0.02
Temperature (kelvin)> 300
Initial volume (milliliters)> 400
Final volume (milliliters)> 600
Volume increment (milliliters)> 50
```

Output File

```
0.0200 moles of carbon dioxide at 300 kelvin
```

Volume (ml)	Pressure (atm)
400	1.2246
450	1.0891
500	0.9807
550	0.8918
600	0.8178

10. A concrete channel to bring water to Crystal Lake is being designed. It will have vertical walls and be 15 feet wide. It will be 10 feet deep, have a slope of .0015 feet/foot, and a roughness coefficient of .014. How deep will the water be when 1,000 cubic feet per second is flowing through the channel? To solve this problem, we can use Manning's equation

$$Q = \frac{1.486}{N} AR^{2/3}S^{1/2}$$

where Q is the flow of water (cubic feet per second), N is the roughness coefficient (unitless), A is the area (square feet), S is the slope (feet/foot), and R is the hydraulic radius (feet).

The hydraulic radius is the cross-sectional area divided by the wetted perimeter. For square channels like the one in this example,

Hydraulic radius = depth × width / (2.0 × depth + width)

To solve this problem, design a program that allows the user to guess a depth and then calculates the corresponding flow. If the flow is too little, the user should guess a depth a little higher; if the flow is too high, the user should guess a depth a little lower. The guessing is repeated until the computed flow is within 0.1 percent of the flow desired.

To help the user make an initial guess, the program should display the flow for half the channel depth. Note the example run:

```
At a depth of 5.0000 feet, the flow is 641.3255 cubic
feet per second.

Enter your initial guess for the channel depth
when the flow is 1000.0000 cubic feet per second
Enter guess> 6.0

Depth: 6.0000  Flow: 825.5906 cfs  Target: 1000.0000 cfs
Difference: 174.4094  Error: 17.4409 percent
Enter guess> 7.0

Depth: 7.0000  Flow: 1017.7784 cfs  Target: 1000.0000 cfs
Difference: -17.7784  Error: -1.7778 percent

Enter guess> 6.8
```

11. Bunyan Lumber Co. needs to create a table of the engineering properties of its lumber. The dimensions of the wood are given as the base and the height in inches. Engineers need to know the following information about lumber:

cross-sectional area: *base × height*

moment of inertia: $\dfrac{base \times height^3}{12}$

section modulus: $\dfrac{base \times height^2}{6}$

The owner makes lumber with base sizes of 2, 4, 6, 8, and 10 inches. The height sizes are 2, 4, 6, 8, 10, and 12 inches. Produce a table with appropriate headings to show these values and the computed engineering properties. The first part of the table's outline is shown.

```
Lumber          Cross-Sectional      Moment of      Section
Size            Area                 Inertia        Modulus

2 x  2
2 x  4
2 x  6
2 x  8
2 x 10
2 x 12
4 x  2
4 x  4
   .
   .
   .
```

12. Before high-resolution graphics displays became common, computer terminals were often used to display graphs of equations using only text characters. A typical technique was to create a vertical graph by spacing over on the screen, then displaying an *. Write a program that displays the graph of an increasing frequency sine wave this way. The program should ask the user for an initial step-size in degrees and the number of lines of the graph to display. A sample output begins as follows:

```
   *
              *
                *
                  *
                    *
                      *
                        *
                         *
                        *
                      *
                    *
                  *
                *
              *
         *
      *
    *
  *
 *
```

Turn the book 90° to see the sine wave shape.

CHAPTER 6

Modular Programming

Quick-Check Exercises

1. The items passed in a function call are the _____ _____. The corresponding _____ _____ appear in the function prototype and heading.
2. Constants and expressions can be actual arguments corresponding to formal parameters that are _____ parameters.
3. Formal parameters that are output parameters must have actual arguments that are _____.
4. Which of the following is used to test a function: a driver or a stub?
5. Which of the following is used to test program flow in a partially complete system: a driver or a stub?
6. The part of a program where an identifier can be referenced is called the _____ of the identifier.
7. What are the values of main function variables x and y at the point marked /* values here */ in the following program?

```
/* nonsense */
void silly(int x);
```

```
int
main(void)
{
        int x, y;

        x = 10; y = 11;
        silly(x);
        silly(y);    /* values here */
              . . .

}

void
silly(int x)
{
        int y;

        y = x + 2;
        x *= 2;
}
```

8. Let's make some changes in our nonsense program. What are main's x and y at /* values here */ in the following version?

```
/* nonsense */
void silly(int *x);

int
main(void)
{
     int x, y;

     x = 10;    y = 11;
     silly(&x);
     silly(&y);   /* values here */
       . . .
}

void
silly(int *x)
{

     int y;

     y = *x + 2;
     *x = 2 * *x;
}
```

Answers to Quick-Check Exercises

1. actual arguments; formal parameters
2. input
3. addresses of variables/pointers
4. driver
5. stub
6. scope
7. x is 10, y is 11
8. x is 20, y is 22

Review Questions

1. Write a function called `letter_grade` that has a type `int` input parameter called `points` and returns through an output parameter `gradep` the appropriate letter grade using a straight scale (90–100 is an A, 80–89 is a B, and so on). Return through a second output parameter (`just_missedp`) an indication of whether the student just missed the next higher grade (true for 89, 79, and so on).
2. Why would you choose to write a function that computes a single numeric or character value as a non `void` function that returns a result through a `return` statement rather than to write a `void` function with an output parameter?
3. Explain the allocation of memory cells when a function is called. What is stored in the function data area for an input parameter? Answer the same question for an output parameter.
4. Which of the functions in the following program outline *can* call the function `grumpy`? All function prototypes and declarations are shown; only executable statements are omitted.

```
int grumpy(int dopey);

char silly(double grumpy);

double happy(int goofy, char greedy);
```

```
int
main(void)
{
        double p, q, r;
        . . .
}

int
grumpy(int dopey)
{
        double silly;
        . . .
}

char
silly(double grumpy)
{
        double happy;
        . . .
}

double
happy(int goofy, char greedy)
{
        char grumpy;
        . . .
}
```

5. Sketch the data areas of functions main and silly as they appear immediately before the return from the first call to silly in Quick-Check Exercise 8.

6. Present arguments against these statements:

   a. It is foolish to use function subprograms because a program written with functions has many more lines than the same program written without functions.

   b. The use of function subprograms leads to more errors because of mistakes in using argument lists.

Programming Projects

1. Write a program for an automatic teller machine that dispenses money. The user should enter the amount desired (a multiple of 10 dollars) and the machine dispenses this amount using the least number of bills. The bills dis-

pensed are 50s, 20s, and 10s. Write a function that determines how many of each kind of bill to dispense.

2. A hospital supply company wants to market a program to assist with the calculation of intravenous rates. Design and implement a program that interacts with the user as follows:

```
INTRAVENOUS RATE ASSISTANT

Enter the number of the problem you wish to solve.
     GIVEN A MEDICAL ORDER IN            CALCULATE RATE IN
(1) ml/hr & tubing drop factor           drops / min
(2) 1 L for n hr                         ml / hr
(3) mg/kg/hr & concentration in mg/ml    ml / hr
(4) units/hr & concentration in units/ml ml / hr
(5) QUIT


Problem=> 1
Enter rate in ml/hr=> 150
Enter tubing's drop factor(drops/ml)=> 15
The drop rate per minute is 38.

Enter the number of the problem you wish to solve.
     GIVEN A MEDICAL ORDER IN            CALCULATE RATE IN
(1) ml/hr & tubing drop factor           drops / min
(2) 1 L for n hr                         ml / hr
(3) mg/kg/hr & concentration in mg/ml    ml / hr
(4) units/hr & concentration in units/ml ml / hr
(5) QUIT


Problem=> 2
Enter number of hours=> 8
The rate in milliliters per hour is 125.

Enter the number of the problem you wish to solve.
     GIVEN A MEDICAL ORDER IN            CALCULATE RATE IN
(1) ml/hr & tubing drop factor           drops / min
(2) 1 L for n hr                         ml / hr
(3) mg/kg/hr & concentration in mg/ml    ml / hr
(4) units/hr & concentration in units/ml ml / hr
(5) QUIT


Problem=> 3
Enter rate in mg/kg/hr=> 0.6
Enter patient weight in kg=> 70
Enter concentration in mg/ml=> 1
The rate in milliliters per hour is 42.


Enter the number of the problem you wish to solve.
```

```
        GIVEN A MEDICAL ORDER IN                CALCULATE RATE IN
(1) ml/hr & tubing drop factor                  drops / min
(2) 1 L for n hr                                ml / hr
(3) mg/kg/hr & concentration in mg/ml           ml / hr
(4) units/hr & concentration in units/ml        ml / hr
(5) QUIT


Problem=> 4
Enter rate in units/hr=> 1000
Enter concentration in units/ml=> 25
The rate in milliliters per hour is 40.

Enter the number of the problem you wish to solve.
        GIVEN A MEDICAL ORDER IN                CALCULATE RATE IN
(1) ml/hr & tubing drop factor                  drops / min
(2) 1 L for n hr                                ml / hr
(3) mg/kg/hr & concentration in mg/ml           ml / hr
(4) units/hr & concentration in units/ml        ml / hr
(5) QUIT


Problem=> 5
```

Implement the following functions:

get_problem—Displays the user menu, then inputs and returns as the function value the problem number selected.

get_rate_drop_factor—Prompts the user to enter the data required for problem 1, and sends this data back to the calling module via output parameters.

get_kg_rate_conc—Prompts the user to enter the data required for problem 3, and sends this data back to the calling module via output parameters.

get_units_conc—Prompts the user to enter the data required for problem 4, and sends this data back to the calling module via output parameters.

fig_drops_min—Takes rate and drop factor as input parameters and returns drops/min (rounded to nearest whole drop) as function value.

fig_ml_hr—Takes as an input parameter the number of hours over which one liter is to be delivered and returns ml/hr (rounded) as function value.

by_weight—Takes as input parameters rate in mg/kg/hr, patient weight in kg, and concentration of drug in mg/ml and returns ml/hr (rounded) as function value.

by_units—Takes as input parameters rate in units/hr and concentration in units/ml, and returns ml/hr(rounded) as function value.

(*Hint:* Use a sentinel-controlled loop. Call `get_problem` once before the loop to initialize the problem number and once again at the end of the loop body to update it.)

3. Write a program to dispense change. The user enters the amount paid and the amount due. The program determines how many dollars, quarters, dimes, nickels, and pennies should be given as change. Write a function with four output parameters that determines the quantity of each kind of coin.

4. The table below summarizes three commonly used mathematical models of nonvertical straight lines.

Mode	Equation	Given
Two-point form	$m = \dfrac{y_2 - y_1}{x_2 - x_1}$	$(x_1, y_1), (x_2, y_2)$
Point-slope form	$y - y_1 = m(x - x_1)$	$m, (x_1, y_1)$
Slope-intercept form	$y = mx + b$	m, b

Design and implement a program that permits the user to convert either two-point form or point-slope form into slope-intercept form. Your program should interact with the user as follows:

```
Select the form that you would like to convert to slope-
intercept form:
1) Two-point form (you know two points on the line)
2) Point-slope form (you know the line's slope and one point)
=> 2

Enter the slope=> 4.2
Enter the x-y coordinates of the point separated by a space=> 1 1

Point-slope form
   y - 1.00 = 4.20(x - 1.00)

Slope-intercept form
   y = 4.20x - 3.20

Do another conversion (Y or N)=> Y
```

```
Select the form that you would like to convert to slope-
intercept form:
1) Two-point form (you know two points on the line)
2) Point-slope form (you know the line's slope and one point)
=> 1

Enter the x-y coordinates of the first point separated by a
space=> 4 3
Enter the x-y coordinates of the second point separated by a
space=> -2 1

Two-point form
       (1.00 - 3.00)
  m = ---------------
       (-2.00 - 4.00)

Slope-intercept form
  y = 0.33x + 1.66

Do another conversion (Y or N)=> N
```

Implement the following functions:

get_problem—Displays the user menu, then inputs and returns as the function value the problem number selected.

get2_pt—Prompts the user for the x-y coordinates of both points, inputs the four coordinates, and returns them to the calling function through output parameters.

get_pt_slope—Prompts the user for the slope and x-y coordinates of the point, inputs the three values and returns them to the calling function through output parameters.

slope_intcpt_from2_pt—Takes four input parameters, the x-y coordinates of two points, and returns through output parameters the slope (m) and y-intercept (b).

intcpt_from_pt_slope—Takes three input parameters, the x-y coordinates of one point and the slope, and returns as the function value the y-intercept.

display2_pt—Takes four input parameters, the x-y coordinates of two points, and displays the two-point line equation with a heading.

display_pt_slope—Takes three input parameters, the x-y coordinates of one point and the slope, and displays the point-slope line equation with a heading.

display_slope_intcpt—Takes two input parameters, the slope and y-intercept, and displays the slope-intercept line equation with a heading.

5. Determine the following information about each value in a list of positive integers.

    a. Is the value a multiple of 7, 11, or 13?
    b. Is the sum of the digits odd or even?
    c. Is the value a prime number?

    You should write a function with three type `int` output parameters that send back the answers to these three questions. Some sample input data might be:

    ```
    104   3773   13   121   77   30751
    ```

6. Develop a collection of functions to solve simple conduction problems using various forms of the formula

    $$H = \frac{kA(T_2 - T_1)}{X}$$

    where H is the rate of heat transfer in watts, k is the coefficient of thermal conductivity for the particular substance, A is the cross-sectional area in m² (square meters), T_2 and T_1 are the kelvin temperatures on the two sides of the conductor, and X is the thickness of the conductor in meters.

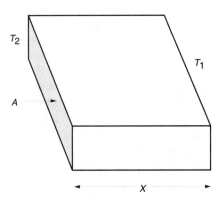

    Define a function for each variable in the formula. For example, function `calc_h` would compute the rate of heat transfer, `calc_k` would figure the coefficient of thermal conductivity, `calc_a` would find the cross-sectional area, and so on.
    Develop a driver function that interacts with the user in the following way:

    ```
    Respond to the prompts with the data known.  For the
    unknown quantity, enter a question mark (?).
    ```

```
Rate of heat transfer (watts) >> 755.0
Coefficient of thermal conductivity (W/m-K) >> 0.8
Cross-sectional area of conductor (m^2) >> 0.12
Temperature on one side (K) >> 298
Temperature on other side (K) >> ?
Thickness of conductor (m) >> 0.003
               kA (T2 - T1)
    H  =   ----------------
                    X
Temperature on the other side is 274 K.
```

```
H = 755.0 W              T2 = 298 K
k = 0.800 W/m-K          T1 = 274 K
A = 0.120 m^2            X  = 0.0003 m
```

(*Hint:* Input of the question mark when looking for a number will cause scanf to return a value of 0. Be sure to check for this, and then scan the question mark into a character variable before proceeding with the remaining prompts.)

7. The square root of a number N can be approximated by repeated calculation using the formula

$$NG = 0.5(LG + N/LG)$$

where NG stands for next guess and LG stands for last guess. Write a function that calculates the square root of a number using this method.

The initial guess will be the starting value of LG. The program will compute a value for NG using the formula given. The difference between NG and LG is checked to see whether these two guesses are almost identical. If they are, NG is accepted as the square root; otherwise, the new guess (NG) becomes the last guess (LG) and the process is repeated (another value is computed for NG, the difference is checked, and so on). The loop should be repeated until the difference is less than 0.005. Use an initial guess of 1.0.

Write a driver function and test your square root function for the numbers 4, 120.5, 88, 36.01, 10,000, and 0.25.

8. The electric company charges according to the following rate schedule:

9 cents per kilowatt-hour (kwh) for the first 300 kwh
8 cents per kwh for the next 300 kwh (up to 600 kwh)
6 cents per kwh for the next 400 kwh (up to 1,000 kwh)
5 cents per kwh for all electricity used over 1,000 kwh

Write a function to compute the total charge for each customer. Write a main function to call the charge calculation function using the following data:

Customer Number	Kilowatt-hours Used
123	725
205	115
464	600
596	327
601	915
613	1,011
722	47

The program should print a three-column chart listing the customer number, the kilowatt-hours used, and the charge for each customer. The program should also compute and print the number of customers, the total kilowatt-hours used, and the total charges.

9. When an aircraft or an automobile is moving through the atmosphere, it must overcome a force called *drag* that works against the motion of the vehicle. The drag force can be expressed as

$$F = \frac{1}{2} CD \times A \times \rho \times V^2$$

where F is the force (in newtons), CD is the drag coefficient, A is the projected area of the vehicle perpendicular to the velocity vector (in m²), ρ is the density of the gas or fluid through which the body is traveling (kg/m³), and V is the body's velocity. The drag coefficient CD has a complex derivation and is frequently an empirical quantity. Sometimes the drag coefficient has its own dependencies on velocities: For an automobile, the range is from approximately 0.2 (for a very streamlined vehicle) through about 0.5. For simplicity, assume a streamlined passenger vehicle is moving through air at sea level (where $\rho = 1.23$ kg/m³). Write a program that allows a user to input A and CD interactively and calls a function to compute and return the drag force. Your program should call the drag force function repeatedly and display a table showing the drag force for the input shape for a range of velocities from 0 m/s to 40 m/s in increments of 5 m/s.

10. Write a program to model a simple calculator. Each data line should consist of the next operation to be performed from the list below and the right operand. Assume the left operand is the accumulator value (initial value of 0). You need a function scan_data with two output parameters that returns the operator and right operand scanned from a data line. You need a function do_next_op that performs the required operation. do_next_op has two

input parameters (the operator and operand) and one input/output parameter (the accumulator). The valid operators are:

+   add
-      subtract
*   multiply
/   divide
^   power (raise left operand to power of right operand)
q   quit

Your calculator should display the accumulator value after each operation. A sample run follows.

```
+ 5.0
result so far is 5.0
^ 2
result so far is 25.0
/ 2.0
result so far is 12.5
q 0
final result is 12.5
```

11. Write a function that computes and displays a table of negative powers of two (2^{-1}, 2^{-2}, and so on) as both common fractions and decimals as shown next. The range of powers printed should be determined by the function's input arguments. Test your function using a driver.

Power of 2	Fraction	Decimal Value
−1	$\frac{1}{2}$	0.5000
−2	$\frac{1}{4}$	0.2500
−3	$\frac{1}{8}$	0.1250

CHAPTER 7

Simple Data Types

Quick-Check Exercises

1. Assuming an ASCII character set, evaluate these expressions.
   a. `(char)((int)'z' - 2)`
   b. `(int)'F' - (int)'A'`
   c. `(char)(5 + (int)'M')`

2. What does this segment print?

```
for   (ch = (int)'d';
        ch < (int)'n';
        ch += 3)
    printf("%c", (char)ch);
printf("\n");
```

3. Which of the following can be an enumeration constant?

   a. an integer
   b. a floating-point number
   c. an identifier
   d. a string value

4. Why is it possible that the following C expression will not evaluate to 1 (true)?

   `(0.1 + 0.1 + 0.1 + 0.1 + 0.1 == 0.5)`

5. What is wrong with the following enumerated type definition?

```
typedef enum
        {2, 3, 5, 7, 11, 13}
prime_t;
```

6. Consider this enumerated type definition:

```
typedef enum
        {frosh, soph, jr, sr}
class_t;
```

What is the value of each of the following?

a. `(int)sr`
b. `(class_t)0`
c. `(class_t)((int)soph + 1)`

What is displayed by this code fragment?

```
for (class = frosh;  class <= sr;  ++class)
    printf("%d  ", class);
printf("\n");
```

7. If this condition is true, what kind of error has occurred?

```
87654321.0 + 0.000123 == 87654321.0
```

8. If the value of the expression

```
32120 + 1000
```

is a negative number, what kind of error has occurred?

9. Consider this enumerated type definition:

```
typedef enum
        {jan, feb, mar, apr, may, jun, jul,
         aug, sep, oct, nov, dec}
month_t;
```

Write a function `next_month` that takes a `month_t` parameter and returns the type `month_t` abbreviation that follows: Let `jan` follow `dec`.

Answers to Quick-Check Exercises

1. a. `'x'`
   b. 5
   c. `'R'`
2. `dgjm`

3. c. an identifier
4. Because of representational error, the fraction 0.1 cannot be represented exactly in binary.
5. Integers cannot be enumerated type values.
6. a. 3
   b. `frosh`
   c. `jr`

   `0  1  2  3`
7. cancellation error
8. arithmetic overflow
9.
```
month_t
next_month(month_t this_month)
{
      month_t next;

      if (this_month == dec)
            next = jan;
      else
            next = (month_t)((int)this_month + 1);

      return (next);
}
```

Review Questions

1. What are the advantages of data type `int` over data type `double`? What are the advantages of type `double` over type `int`?
2. List and explain three computational errors that may occur in type `double` expressions.
3. Assume you are using the ASCII character set, and write a `for` loop that runs from the code for `'z'` down to the code for `'A'` and prints only the consonants. Define a function `is_vowel` that returns a `1` if its character argument is a vowel and a `0` otherwise. Call this function from your loop.
4. Write a C function with type `int` argument n and type `double` argument x that returns as its value the sum of the first n terms of the series

$$x + \frac{x^2}{2} + \frac{x^3}{3} + \frac{x^4}{4} + \ldots + \frac{x^n}{n}$$

5. Write a function for displaying (as a string) a value of enumerated type `season_t`:

```
typedef enum
      {winter, spring, summer, fall}
season_t;
```

6. Define an enumerated type `fiscal_t` as the months from July through June. Declare a variable named `month` of type `fiscal_t`, and write a `switch` statement controlled by `month` that displays `"summer"` for `june`, `july`, and `august`; `"fall"` for `september`, `october`, `november`; `"winter"` for `december`, `january`, `february`; `"spring"` for `march`, `april`, `may`; and `"invalid month"` for other values.

7. Write a `for` loop that would display

   ```
   0.1   0.2   0.3   0.4   0.5   0.6   0.7   0.8   0.9   1.0
   ```

   for *all* C implementations.

8. If the maximum value representable as an `int` were 32,767, which of the following values would likely be the maximum value representable as type `unsigned` in the same implementation?

   a. 32,767   b. 45,000   c. 65,534   d. 75,767

9. An explicit conversion from one data type to another is called a _____ .

Programming Projects

1. Write a program that computes the sum

$$s = \sum_{i=1}^{1000} x \qquad \text{where } x = 0.1$$

   Compute this sum twice: once with the variables for *s* and *x* declared `float`, once with the variables declared `double`. Calculate the error in each sum $(100.0 - s)$. You may wish to use these declarations:

   ```
   float  sf, xf = 0.1f;
   double sd, xd = 0.1;
   ```

2. Write a program using loops that demonstrates the problem of representational error. For each fraction from $\frac{1}{2}$ to $\frac{1}{30}$, add up *n* copies of $\frac{1}{n}$ and then compare the sum to 1. If the sum is equal to 1, display a line such as

   ```
   Adding n  1/n's gives a result of 1.
   ```

   If not, display either

   ```
   Adding n  1/n's gives a result less than 1.
   ```

   or

   ```
   Adding n  1/n's gives a result greater than 1.
   ```

   Use nested loops—an outer loop that counts from 2 to 30 and an inner loop that adds up $\frac{1}{2} + \frac{1}{2}$ on the first iteration of the outer loop, $\frac{1}{3} + \frac{1}{3} + \frac{1}{3}$ on the second iteration, and so on.

3. The rate of decay of a radioactive isotope is given in terms of its half-life *H*, the time lapse required for the isotope to decay to one-half of its original mass. The isotope strontium-90 (^{90}Sr) has a half-life of 28 years. Compute and print in table form the amount of this isotope that remains after each year for *n* years, given the initial presence of an amount in grams. The values of *n* and *amount* should be provided interactively. The amount of ^{90}Sr remaining can be computed by using the following formula:

$$r = amount \times C^{(y/H)}$$

where *amount* is the initial amount in grams, *C* is expressed as $e^{-0.693}$ (e = 2.71828), *y* is the number of years elapsed, and *H* is the half-life of the isotope in years.

4. The value for π can be determined by the series equation

$$\pi = 4 \times \left(1 - \frac{1}{3} + \frac{1}{5} - \frac{1}{7} + \frac{1}{9} - \frac{1}{11} + \frac{1}{13} - \cdots\right)$$

Write a program to approximate the value of π using the formula given including terms up through 1/99.

5. In this chapter we studied the bisection method for finding a root of an equation. Another method for finding a root, Newton's method, usually converges to a solution even faster than the bisection method, if it converges at all. Newton's method starts with an initial guess for a root, x_0, and then generates successive approximate roots $x_1, x_2, \ldots, x_j, x_{j+1}, \ldots$, using the iterative formula

$$x_{j+1} = x_j - \frac{f(x_j)}{f'(x_j)}$$

where $f'(x_j)$ is the derivative of function *f* evaluated at $x = x_j$. The formula generates a new guess, x_{j+1}, from a previous one, x_j. Sometimes Newton's method will fail to converge to a root. In this case, the program should terminate after many trials, perhaps 100.

Figure 7.12 shows the geometric interpretation of Newton's method where x_0, x_1, and x_2 represent successive guesses for the root. At each point x_j, the derivative, $f'(x_j)$, is the slope of the tangent to the curve, $f(x)$. The next guess for the root, x_{j+1}, is the point at which the tangent crosses the *x* axis.

From geometry, we get the equation

$$\frac{y_{j+1} - y_j}{x_{j+1} - x_j} = m$$

where *m* is the slope of the line between points (x_{j+1}, y_{j+1}) and (x_j, y_j). In Fig. 7.12, we see that y_{j+1} is zero, y_j is $f(x_j)$, and *m* is $f'(x_j)$; therefore by substituting and rearranging terms, we get

$$-f(x_j) = f'(x_j) \times (x_{j+1} - x_j)$$

leading to the formula shown at the beginning of this problem.

FIGURE 7.12

Geometric
Interpretation of
Newton's Method

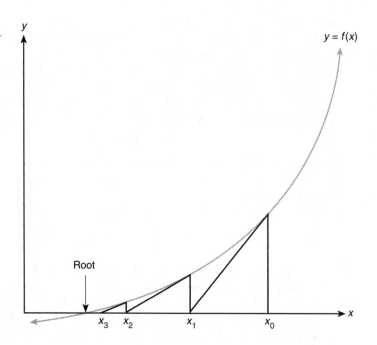

Write a program that uses Newton's method to approximate the nth root of a number to six decimal places. If $x^n = c$, then $x^n - c = 0$. Finding a root of the second equation will give you $\sqrt[n]{c}$. Test your program on $\sqrt{2}$, $\sqrt[3]{7}$, and $\sqrt[3]{-1}$. Your program could use $c/2$ as its initial guess.

6. You would like to find the area under the curve

$$y = f(x)$$

between the lines $x = a$ and $x = b$. One way to approximate this area is to use line segments as approximations of small pieces of the curve and then to sum the areas of trapezoids created by drawing perpendiculars from the line segment endpoints to the x-axis, as shown in Fig. 7.13. We will assume that $f(x)$ is nonnegative over the interval $[a,b]$. The trapezoidal rule approximates this area T as

$$T = \frac{h}{2} \left(f(a) + f(b) + 2 \sum_{i=1}^{n-1} f(x_i) \right)$$

for n subintervals of length h:

$$h = \frac{b-a}{n}$$

FIGURE 7.13

Approximating the
Area Under a
Curve with
Trapezoids

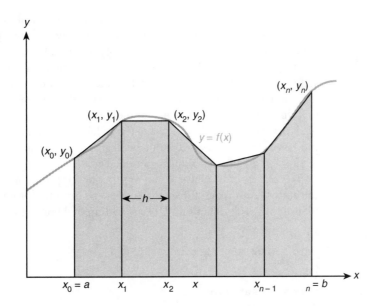

Write a function `trap` with input parameters a, b, n, and f that implements
the trapezoidal rule. Call `trap` with values for n of 2, 4, 8, 16, 32, 64, and 128
on functions

$$g(x) = x^2 \sin x \qquad (a = 0, b = 3.14159)$$

and

$$h(x) = \sqrt{4 - x^2} \qquad (a = -2, b = 2)$$

Function h defines a half-circle of radius 2. Compare your approximation to
the actual area of this half-circle.

Note: If you have studied calculus, you will observe that the trapezoidal rule
is approximating

$$\int_a^b f(x)dx$$

7. Since communications channels are often noisy, numerous ways have been
devised to ensure reliable data transmission. One successful method uses a
checksum. A checksum for a message can be computed by summing the integer codes of the characters in the message and finding the remainder of this
sum divided by 64. The integer code for a space character is added to this
result to obtain the checksum. Since this value is within the range of the dis-
playable characters, it is displayed as a character as well. Write a program
that accepts single-line messages ending with a period and displays the

checksum character for each message. Your program should continue displaying checksums until the user enters a line with only a period.

8. A finite state machine (FSM) consists of a set of states, a set of transitions, and a string of input data. In the FSM of Fig. 7.14, the named ovals represent states, and the arrows connecting the states represent transitions. The FSM is designed to recognize a list of C identifiers and nonnegative integers, assuming that the items are ended by one or more blanks and that a period marks the end of all the data. The following table traces how the diagrammed machine would process a string composed of one blank, the digits 9 and 5, two blanks, the letter K, the digit 9, one blank, and a period. The machine begins in the start state.

Write a program that uses an enumerated type to represent the names of the states. Your program should process a correctly formatted line of data, identifying each data item. Here is a sample of correct input and output.

Input:
```
rate  R2D2 48   2 time    555666 .
```

Output:
```
rate — Identifier
R2D2 — Identifier
48 — Number
2 — Number
time — Identifier
555666 — Number
```

FIGURE 7.14

Finite State
Machine for
Numbers and
Identifiers

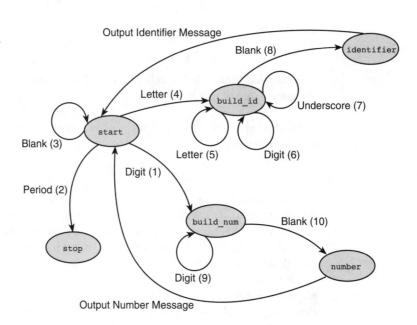

Trace of Fig. 7.12 FSM on data " 95   K9 ."

State	Next Character	Transition
start	' '	3
start	'9'	1
build_num	'5'	9
build_num	' '	10
number		Output number message
start	' '	3
start	'K'	4
build_id	'9'	6
build_id	' '	8
identifier		Output identifier message
start	'.'	2
stop		

Use the following code fragment in main, and design function transition to return the next state for all the numbered transitions of the finite state machine. If you include the header file ctype.h, you can use the library function isdigit which returns 1 if called with a digit character, 0 otherwise. Similarly, the function isalpha checks whether a character is a letter. When your program correctly models the behavior of the FSM shown, extend the FSM and your program to allow optional signs and optional fractional parts (i.e., a decimal point followed by zero or more digits) in numbers.

```
current_state = start;
do {
    if (current_state == identifier) {
        printf(" - Identifier\n");
        current_state = start;
    } else if (current_state == number) {
        printf(" - Number\n");
        current_state = start;
    }
    scanf("%c", &transition_char);
    if (transition_char != ' ')
        printf("%c", transition_char);
    current_state = transition(current_state,
                                transition_char);
} while (current_state != stop);
```

CHAPTER 8

Arrays

Quick-Check Exercises

1. What is a data structure?

2. Of what data type are array subscripting expressions?
3. Can two elements of the same array be of different data types?
4. If an array is declared to have 10 elements, must the program use all ten?
5. The two methods of array access are called _____and _____ .
6. An _____ loop allows us to access easily the elements of an array in _____ order.
7. What is the difference in the use of array b that is implied by these two prototypes?

```
int fun_one(int b[], n)    ;
int fun_two(const int b[], n);
```

8. Look again at the prototypes in Exercise 7. Why does neither array declaration indicate a size?
9. Let nums be an array of 12 type int locations. Describe how the following loop works.

```
i = 0;
for (status = scanf("%d", &n);
        status == 1  &&  i < 12;
        status = scanf("%d", &n))
      nums[i++] = n;
```

10. How many elements does array m have? Show how you would reference each one.

```
double m[2][4];
```

11. If x is an array declared

```
int x[10];
```

and you see a function call such as

```
some_fun(x, n);
```

how can you tell whether x is an input or an output argument?

Answers to Quick-Check Exercises

1. A data structure is a grouping of related values in main memory.
2. type int
3. no
4. no
5. sequential, random
6. indexed, sequential

7. In `fun_one`, b can be used as an output parameter or as an input/output parameter. In `fun_two`, b is strictly an input parameter array.

8. The size of b is not needed because the function does not allocate storage for copying parameter arrays. Only the starting address of the actual argument array will be stored in the formal parameter.

9. As long as `scanf` continues to return a value of 1 meaning a valid integer has been obtained for n, unless the subscript i is $\geq$ 12, the loop body will store the input in the next element of `nums` and will increment the loop counter. The loop exits on EOF (`scanf` returns a negative value), on invalid data (`scanf` returns zero), or on i no longer being less than 12.

10. m has eight elements: `m[0][0]`, `m[0][1]`, `m[0][2]`, `m[0][3]`, `m[1][0]`, `m[1][1]`, `m[1][2]`, `m[1][3]`.

11. You can't tell by looking at the function call, nor can you rely on the proto-type of `some_fun` to tell you either unless the corresponding formal param-eter declaration has a `const` qualifier. If it does, x must be an input argument.

Review Questions

1. Identify an error in the following C statements:

```
int x[8], i;
for  (i = 0;  i <= 8;  ++i)
    x[i] = i;
```

Will the error be detected? If so, when?

2. Declare an array of type `double` values called `exper` that can be referenced by using any day of the week as a subscript, where 0 represents Sunday, 1 represents Monday, and so on.

3. The statement marked `/* this one */` in the following code is valid. True or false?

```
int counts[10], i;
double x[5];
printf("Enter an integer between 0 and 4> ");
i = 0;
scanf("%d", &counts[i]);
x[counts[i]] = 8.384;  /* this one */
```

4. What are the two common ways of selecting array elements for processing?

5. Write a C program segment to display the index of the smallest and the largest numbers in an array x of 20 integers. Assume array x already has val-ues assigned to each element.

6. Write a C function called `reverse` that takes an array named x as an input parameter and an array named y as an output parameter. A third function parameter is n, the number of values in x. The function should copy the integers in x into y but in reverse order (i.e., `y[0]` gets `x[n - 1]`, ... `y[n - 1]` gets `x[0]`).

7. Write a program segment to display the sum of the values in each row of a 5 × 3 type `double` array named `table`. How many row sums will be displayed? How many elements are included in each sum?

8. Answer Review Question 7 for the column sums.

Programming Projects

1. Write a program to grade an *n*-question multiple-choice exam (for *n* between 10 and 50) and provide feedback about the most frequently missed questions. Your program will take data from the file `examdat.txt`. The first line of the file contains the number of questions on the exam followed by a space and then an *n*-character string of the correct answers. Write a function `fgetAnswers` that inputs the answers from an open input file. Each of the lines that follow contain an integer student ID followed by a space and then that student's answers. Function `fgetAnswers` can also be called to input a student's answers. Your program is to produce an output file, `report.txt`, containing the answer key, each student's ID and each student's score as a percentage, and then information about how many students missed each question. Here are short sample input and output files.

examdat.txt
```
5 dbbac
111 dabac
102 dcbdc
251 dbbac
```

report.txt
```
        Exam Report

Question  1  2  3  4  5
Answer    d  b  b  a  c
```

2. If n points are connected to form a closed polygon as shown below, the area A of the polygon can be computed as

$$A = \frac{1}{2}\left|\sum_{i=0}^{n-2}\left(x_{i+1}+x_i\right)\left(y_{i+1}-y_i\right)\right|$$

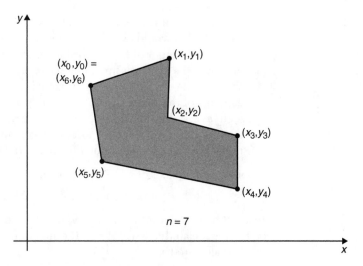

Notice that although the illustrated polygon has only six distinct corners, n for this polygon is 7 because the algorithm expects that the last point, (x_6, y_6), will be a repeat of the initial point, (x_0, y_0).

Represent the (x, y) coordinates of the connected points as two arrays of at most 20 type **double** values. For one of your tests, use the following data set, which defines a polygon whose area is 25.5 square units.

x	y
4	0
4	7.5
7	7.5
7	3
9	0
7	0
4	0

Implement the following functions:

get_corners—Takes as parameters an input file, arrays x and y, and the arrays' maximum size. Fills the arrays with data from the file (ignoring any data that would overflow the arrays) and returns as the function value the number of (x, y) coordinates stored in the arrays.

output_corners—Takes as parameters an output file and two type double arrays of the same size and their actual size, and outputs to the file the contents of the two arrays in two columns.

polygon_area—Takes as parameters two arrays representing the (x, y) coordinates of the corners of a closed polygon and their actual size and returns as the function value the area of the closed polygon.

3. A point mass consists of a 3-D location and an associated mass, such as

Location: (6, 0, -2)   Mass: 3g

In a system of point masses, let $p_1, p_2, ... p_n$ be the n 3-D points and $m_1, m_2, ... m_n$ be their associated masses. If m is the sum of the masses, the center of gravity C is calculated as

$$C = \frac{1}{m} (m_1 p_1 + m_2 p_2 + ... + m_n p_n)$$

Write a program that repeatedly inputs point-mass system data sets from an input file until an input operation fails. For each data set, display the location matrix, the mass vector, n, and the center of gravity.

Each data set includes a location matrix (an matrix in which each row is a point), a one-dimensional array of masses, and the number of point masses, n. Allow n to vary from 3 to 10.

Sample Data File

```
4
 5  -4   3   2
 4   3  -2   5
-4  -3  -1   2
-9   8   6   1
```

This sample should be stored as:

```
location   5   -4    3
           4    3   -2
          -4   -3   -1
          -9    8    6
mass       2
           5
           2
           1
n          4
```

Your main function should repeatedly input and process data sets from an input file until end of file is encountered. For each point-mass system data set, display the location matrix, the mass vector, n, and the center of gravity. Implement at least the following functions:

fget_point_mass: Takes an open input file and a maximum value for n as parameters and fills a two-dimensional array output parameter with a location matrix and a one-dimensional array output parameter with a mass vector from the data file. Returns as function value the actual value of n.

center_grav: Takes a location matrix, mass vector, and n value as parameters, and calculates and returns as the function value the center of gravity of the system.

fwrite_point_mass: Takes an open output file and the location matrix, mass vector, and n value of a point-mass system as parameters and writes the system to the file with meaningful labels.

4. Write a program to take two numerical lists of the same length ended by a sentinel value and store the lists in arrays x and y, each of which has 20 elements. Let n be the actual number of data values in each list. Store the product of corresponding elements of x and y in a third array, z, also of size 20. Display the arrays x, y, and z in a three-column table. Then compute and display the square root of the sum of the items in z. Make up your own data, and be sure to test your program on at least one data set with number lists of exactly 20 items. One data set should have lists of 21 numbers, and one set should have significantly shorter lists.

5. Let `arr` be an array of 20 integers. Write a program that first fills the array with up to 20 input values and then finds and displays both the *subscript* of the largest item in `arr` and the value of the largest item.

6. Each year the Department of Traffic Accidents receives accident count reports from a number of cities and towns across the country. To summarize these reports, the department provides a frequency distribution printout that gives the number of cities reporting accident counts in the following ranges: 0–99, 100–199, 200–299, 300–399, 400–499, and 500 or above. The department needs a computer program to take the number of accidents for each reporting city or town and add one to the count for the appropriate accident range. After all the data have been processed, the resulting frequency counts are to be displayed.

7. A normalized vector X is defined as

$$x_i = \frac{v_i}{\sqrt{\sum_{i=1}^{n} v_i^2}} \; ; \qquad i = 1, 2, \ldots, n$$

Each element of the normalized vector X is computed by dividing the corresponding element (v_i) of the original vector by the square root of the sum of the squares of all the original vector's elements. Design and test a program that repeatedly scans and normalizes vectors of different lengths. Define functions `scan_vector`, `normalize_vector`, and `print_vector`.

8. Generate a table that indicates the rainfall for the city of Plainview and compares the current year's rainfall for the city with the rainfall from the previous year. Display some summary statistics that will indicate both the annual rainfall for each year and the average monthly rainfall for each year. The input data will consist of twelve pairs of numbers. The first number in each pair will be the current year's rainfall for a month, and the second number will be what fell during the same month the previous year. The first data pair will represent January, the second will be February, and so forth. If you assume the data begin

```
3.2     4     (for January)
2.2     1.6   (for February)
```

the output should resemble the following:

```
                    Table of monthly rainfall
                   January      February     March . . .
        This year     3.2          2.2
        Last year     4.0          1.6

        Total rainfall this year:  35.7
        Total rainfall last year:  42.8
        Average monthly rainfall for this year:  3.6
        Average monthly rainfall for last year:  4.0
```

9. Write an interactive program that plays a game of hangman. Store the word to be guessed in successive elements of an array of individual characters called word. The player must guess the letters belonging to word. The program should terminate when either all letters have been guessed correctly (the player wins) or a specified number of incorrect guesses have been made (the computer wins). *Hint:* Use another array, guessed, to keep track of the solution so far. Initialize all elements of guessed to the ' * ' symbol. Each time a letter in word is guessed, replace the corresponding ' * ' in guessed with that letter.

10. The results from the mayor's race have been reported by each precinct as follows:

Precinct	Candidate A	Candidate B	Candidate C	Candidate D
1	192	48	206	37
2	147	90	312	21
3	186	12	121	38
4	114	21	408	39
5	267	13	382	29

Write a program to do the following:

a. Display the table with appropriate labels for the rows and columns.
b. Compute and display the total number of votes received by each candidate and the percentage of the total votes cast.
c. If any one candidate received over 50 percent of the votes, the program should display a message declaring that candidate the winner.

d. If no candidate received 50 percent of the votes, the program should display a message declaring a runoff between the two candidates receiving the highest number of votes; the two candidates should be identified by their letter names.

e. Run the program once with the data shown and once with candidate C receiving only 108 votes in Precinct 4.

11. Write a function that will merge the contents of two sorted (ascending order) arrays of type `double` values, storing the result in an array output parameter (still in ascending order). The function should not assume that both its input parameter arrays are the same length but can assume that one array does not contain two copies of the same value. The result array should also contain no duplicate values.

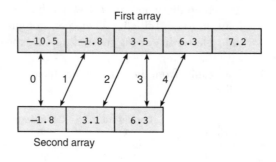

Hint: When one of the input arrays has been exhausted, do not forget to copy the remaining data in the other array into the result array. Test your function with cases in which (1) the first array is exhausted first, (2) the second array is exhausted first, and (3) the two arrays are exhausted at the same time (i.e., they end with the same value). Remember that the arrays input to this function *must already be sorted.*

12. The *binary search* algorithm that follows may be used to search an array when the elements are in order. This algorithm is analogous to the following approach for finding a name in a telephone book.

a. Open the book in the middle, and look at the middle name on the page.

b. If the middle name isn't the one you're looking for, decide whether it comes before or after the name you want.

c. Take the appropriate half of the section of the book you were looking in and repeat these steps until you land on the name.

ALGORITHM FOR BINARY SEARCH

1. Let `bottom` be the subscript of the initial array element.
2. Let `top` be the subscript of the last array element.
3. Let `found` be false.
4. Repeat as long as `bottom` isn't greater than `top` and the target has not been found

    5. Let `middle` be the subscript of the element halfway between `bottom` and `top`.

    6. if the element at `middle` is the target

        7. Set `found` to true and `index` to `middle`.

    else if the element at `middle` is larger than the target

        8. Let `top` be `middle - 1`.

    else

        9. Let `bottom` be `middle + 1`.

Write and test a function `binary_srch` that implements this algorithm for an array of integers. When there is a large number of array elements, which function do you think is faster: `binary_srch` or the linear search function of Fig. 8.15?

13. The *bubble sort* is another technique for sorting an array. A bubble sort compares adjacent array elements and exchanges their values if they are out of order. In this way, the smaller values "bubble" to the top of the array (toward element 0), while the larger values sink to the bottom of the array. After the first pass of a bubble sort, the last array element is in the correct position; after the second pass the last two elements are correct, and so on. Thus, after each pass, the unsorted portion of the array contains one less element. Write and test a function that implements this sorting method.

14. A C program can represent a real polynomial $p(x)$ of degree n as an array of the real coefficients $a_0, a_1, \ldots, a_n$ $(a_n \neq 0)$.

$$p(x) = a_0 + a_1 x + a_2 x^2 + \ldots + a_n x^n$$

Write a program that inputs a polynomial of maximum degree 8 and then evaluates the polynomial at various values of x. Include a function `get_poly` that fills the array of coefficients and sets the degree of the polynomial, and a function `eval_poly` that evaluates a polynomial at a given value of x. Use these function prototypes:

```
void get_poly( double coeff[], int* degreep );
double eval_poly( const double coeff[], int degree,
                  ( double x );
```

15. Peabody Public Utilities tracks the status of its power service throughout the city with a 3 × 4 grid in which each cell represents power service in one sector. When power is available everywhere, all grid values are 1. A grid value of 0 indicates an outage somewhere in the sector.

    Write a program that inputs a grid from a file and displays the grid. If all grid values are 1, display the message

```
Power is on throughout grid.
```

Otherwise, list the sectors that have outages:

```
Power is off in sectors:
    (0,0)
    (1,2)
```

Include in your program functions `get_grid`, `display_grid`, `power_ok`, and `where_off`. Function `power_ok` returns true (1) if power is on in all sectors, false (0) otherwise. Function `where_off` should display the message regarding sectors experiencing outages.

16. The *Game of Life*, invented by John H. Conway, is supposed to model the genetic laws for birth, survival, and death (see *Scientific American*, October 1970, p. 120). We will play the game on a board that consists of 25 squares in the horizontal and vertical directions (a total of 625 squares). Each square can be empty, or it can contain an X indicating the presence of an organism. Each square (except for the border squares) has eight neighbors. The color shading shown in the following segment of the board marks the neighbors of the organism named X*:

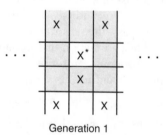

Generation 1

The next generation of organisms is determined according to the following criteria:

a. Birth—an organism will be born in each empty location that has exactly three neighbors.

b. Death—an organism with four or more organisms as neighbors will die from overcrowding. An organism with fewer than two neighbors will die from loneliness.

c. Survival—an organism with two or three neighbors will survive to the next generation. Possible generations 2 and 3 for the sample follow:

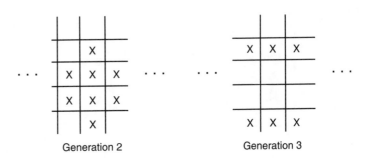

Generation 2   Generation 3

Take an initial configuration of organisms as input data. Display the original game array, calculate the next generation of organisms in a new array, copy the new array into the original game array, and repeat the cycle for as many generations as you wish. *Hint:* Assume that the borders of the game array are infertile regions where organisms can neither survive nor be born; you will not have to process the border squares.

CHAPTER 9

Strings

Quick-Check Exercises

1. For each of the following functions, explain its purpose, the type(s) of its output parameters, and the type(s) of its input parameter(s). Also indicate if it is user-defined or if it is from the string library or from the ctype library.

strcpy	strncpy	strncat
islower	strcat	scanline
isalpha	strlen	strcmp

2. Look at Appendix A, which lists three character sets. Which of the following expressions may yield different results on different computers?

   a. `(char)45`
   b. `'a' < 'A'`
   c. `'A' < 'Z'`
   d. `('A' <= ch && ch <= 'Z') && isalpha(ch)`
   e. `(int)'A'`
   f. `(int)'B' - (int)'A'`

3. Which of the following strings could represent space allocated for a local variable? Which could represent a formal parameter of any length?

   `char str1[50]`   `char str2[]`

4. A program you have written is producing incorrect results on your second data set, although it runs fine on the first. As you debug, you discover that the value of one of your strings is spontaneously changing from `"blue"` to `"al"` in the following code segment. What could be wrong?

```
.  .  .
printf("%s\n", s1);   /* displays "blue" */
scanf("%s", s2);
printf("%s\n", s1);   /* displays "al"   */
.  .  .
```

5. Declare a variable `str` with as little space as would be reasonable given that `str` will hold each of the values below in turn.

```
carbon     uranium     tungsten     bauxite
```

6. What is the value of `t1` after execution of these statements if the value of `t2` is `"Merry Christmas"`?

```
strncpy(t1, &t2[3], 5);    t1[5] = '\0';
```

7. The action of joining two strings is called _____ .
8. Write a statement that assigns to `s1` the end of the string value of `s2` starting with the fourth character (i.e., `s2[3]`).
9. Write statements that take a whole data line as input and display all the uppercase letters in the line.
10. What is the value of the following expression?

```
isdigit(9)
```

11. What does this program fragment display?

```
char city[20] = "Washington DC 20059";
char *one, *two, *three;
one = strtok(city, " ");
two = strtok(NULL, " ");
three = strtok(NULL, " ");
printf("%s\n%s\n%s\n", one, two, three);
```

12. After execution of the fragment in Exercise 11, is the value of `city` still `"Washington DC 20059"`?

Answers to Quick-Check Exercises

1.

Function's Purpose	Output Parameter Types	Input Parameter Types	Where Defined
strcpy copies one string into another.	char * (string result)	const char * (input string)	string
islower checks whether its argument is the character code for a lowercase character.	none	int	ctype
isalpha determines if its argument is the character code for a letter of the alphabet.	none	int	ctype
strncpy copies *n* characters of one string into another.	char * (string result)	const char * (source string) int	string
strcat concatenates one string on the end of another.	char * (input/output argument — first source string and string result)	const char * (second source string)	string
strlen finds the length of its argument, counting the letters that precede the null character.	none	const char * (source string)	string
strncat concatenates two arguments by adding up to *n* characters from the second argument to the end of the first argument.	char * (input/output argument — first source string and string result)	const char * (second source string) int (maximum number of characters to copy from second string)	string

(continued)

Function's Purpose	Output Parameter Types	Input Parameter Types	Where Defined
`scanline` takes one line of input as a string, stores as much as will fit in its output argument, and discards the rest.	`char *` (string result)	`int` (space available in result string)	user
`strcmp` compares arguments and returns a negative integer if first is less than second, zero if they are equal, and a positive integer otherwise	none	`const char *` (2 input strings)	string

2. Results differ for a, b, e.
3. local variable: `str1`;   parameter: `str2`
4. The call to `scanf` may be getting a string too long to fit in `s2`, and the extra characters could be overwriting memory allocated to `s1`.
5. `char str[9]`. The longest value (`"tungsten"`) has eight characters, and one more is needed for the null character.
6. `"ry Ch"`
7. concatenation
8. `strcpy(s1, &s2[3]);`
9. `gets(line);`
```
for  (i = 0;  i < strlen(line);  ++i)
     if (isupper(line[i]))
           putchar(line[i]);
```
10. `0` (false). However, `isdigit('9')` would be true.
11. `Washington`
`DC`
`20059`
12. No.

Review Questions

Refer to these declarations when determining the effect of the statements in Questions 1–4.

```
char s5[5], s10[10], s20[20];
char aday[7] = "Sunday";
char another[9] = "Saturday";
```

1. `strncpy(s5, another, 4); s5[4] = '\0';`
2. `strcpy(s10, &aday[3]);`
3. `strlen(another)`
4. `strcpy(s20, aday); strcat(s20, another);`
5. Write a function that pads a variable-length string with blanks to its maximum size. For example, if `s10` is a ten-character array currently holding the string `"screen"`, `blank_pad` would add three blanks (one of which would overwrite the null character) and finish the string with the null character. Be sure your function would work if no blank padding were necessary.
6. Write a function that would return a copy of its string argument with the first occurrence of a specified letter deleted.
7. Write functions `isvowel` and `isconsonant` that return true if their type `int` argument is the character code for a vowel (or consonant). *Hint:* Use a `switch` statement in `isvowel`.
8. Which one of the following would call `somefun` only if the string values of character arrays a and b were equal?

   a. ```
      if (strcmp(a, b))
            somefun();
      ```
   b. ```
      if (strcmp(a, b) == 0)
            somefun();
      ```
   c. ```
      if (a == b)
            somefun();
      ```
   d. ```
      if (a[] == b[])
            somefun();
      ```

9. What does this program fragment display?

   ```
   char x[80] = "gorilla";
   char y[80] = "giraffe";
   strcpy(x, y);
   printf("%s %s\n", x, y);
   ```

a. gorilla giraffe
b. giraffegorilla gorilla
c. gorilla gorilla
d. giraffe giraffe

10. What does this program fragment display?

```
char x[80] = "gorilla";
char y[80] = "giraffe";
strcat(x, y);
printf("%s %s\n", x, y);
```

a. gorillagiraffe giraffe
b. giraffegorilla gorilla
c. gorilla gorilla
d. giraffe giraffe

Programming Projects

1. Write and test a function `deblank` that takes a string output and a string input argument and returns a copy of the input argument with all blanks removed.

2. A resistor is a circuit device designed to have a specific resistance value between its ends. Resistance values are expressed in ohms (Ω) or kilo-ohms (kΩ). Resistors are frequently marked with colored bands that encode their resistance values, as shown in Fig. 9.23. The first two bands are digits, and the third is a power-of-ten multiplier.

FIGURE 9.23

Bands Encoding
the Resistance
Value of a Resistor

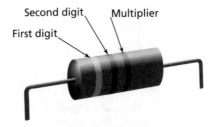

Second digit   Multiplier

First digit

The table below shows the meanings of each band color. For example, if the first band is green, the second is black, and the third is orange, the resistor has a value of $50 \times 10^3 \Omega$ or 50 kΩ. The information in the table can be stored in a C++ program as an array of strings.

```
char COLOR_CODES[10][7] = {"black", "brown", "red",
    "orange", "yellow", "green", "blue", "violet", "gray",
    "white"};
```

Notice that `"red"` is `COLOR_CODES[2]` and has a digit value of 2 and a multiplier value of 10^2. In general, `COLOR_CODES[n]` has digit value n and multiplier value 10^n.

Write a program that prompts for the colors of Band 1, Band 2, and Band 3, and then displays the resistance in kilo-ohms. Include a helper function `search` that takes three parameters—the list of strings, the size of the list, and a target string, and returns the subscript of the list element that matches the target or returns –1 if the target is not in the list. Here is a short sample run:

```
Enter the colors of the resistor's three bands, beginning with
the band nearest the end.  Type the colors in lowercase letters
only, NO CAPS.
```

Coler Codes for Resistors[*]

Color	Value as Digit	Value as Multiplier
Black	0	1
Brown	1	10
Red	2	10^2
Orange	3	10^3
Yellow	4	10^4
Green	5	10^5
Blue	6	10^6
Violet	7	10^7
Gray	8	10^8
White	9	10^9

[*]Adapted from *Sears and Zemansky's University Physics*, 10th edited by Hugh D. Young and Roger A. Freedman (Boston: Addison-Wesley, 2000), p. 807.

```
Band 1 => green
Band 2 => black
Band 3 => yellow
Resistance value:  500 kilo—ohms
Do you want to decode another resistor?
=> y
Enter the colors of the resistor's three bands, beginning with
the band nearest the end.  Type the colors in lowercase letters
only, NO CAPS.
Band 1 => brown
Band 2 => vilet
Band 3 => gray
Invalid color: vilet
Do you want to decode another resistor?
=> n
```

3. Write a program that processes a sequence of lines, displaying a count of the total number of words in those lines as well as counts of the number of words with one letter, two letters, and so on.

4. Write and test a function `hydroxide` that returns a 1 for true if its string argument ends in the substring `OH`.

   Try the function hydroxide on the following data:

   `KOH  H2O2  NaCl  NaOH  C9H8O4  MgOH`

5. Write a program that takes nouns and forms their plurals on the basis of these rules:

   a. If noun ends in "y," remove the "y" and add "ies."
   b. If noun ends in "s," "ch," or "sh," add "es."
   c. In all other cases, just add "s."

   Print each noun and its plural. Try the following data:

   `chair  dairy  boss  circus  fly  dog  church  clue  dish`

6. Write a program that stores lists of names (the last name first) and ages in parallel arrays and sorts the names into alphabetical order keeping the ages with the correct names. Sample output:

```
Original list

----------------------------

        Ryan, Elizabeth     62

    McIntyre, Osborne       84

      DuMond, Kristin       18

          Larson, Lois      42

      Thorpe, Trinity       15

        Ruiz, Pedro         35


Alphabetized list

----------------------------

      DuMond, Kristin       18

          Larson, Lois      42

    McIntyre, Osborne       84

          Ruiz, Pedro       35

      Ryan, Elizabeth       62

      Thorpe, Trinity       15
```

7. Write a program that takes data a line at a time and reverses the words of the line. For example,

```
Input: birds and bees
Reversed: bees and birds
```

The data should have one blank between each pair of words.

8. Write and test a function that finds the longest common prefix of two words (e.g., the longest common prefix of "global" and "glossary" is "glo," of "department" and "depart" is "depart," and of "glove" and "dove" is the empty string).

9. Write a program that processes a data file of names in which each name is on a separate line of at most 80 characters. Here are two sample names:

Hartman-Montgomery, Jane R.
Doe, J. D.

On each line the surname is followed by a comma and a space. Next comes the first name or initial, then a space and the middle initial. Your program should scan the names into three arrays—surname, first, and middle_init. If the surname is longer than 15 characters, store only the first 15. Similarly, limit the first name to 10 characters. Do not store periods in the `first` and `middle_init` arrays. Write the array's contents to a file, aligning the contents of each column:

```
Hartman-Montgom    Jane         R
Doe                J            D
```

CHAPTER 11

Structure and Union Types

Quick-Check Exercises

1. What is the primary difference between a structure and an array? Which would you use to store the catalog description of a course? To store the names of students in the course?

2. How do you access a component of a structure type variable?

   Exercises 3–8 refer to the following type `student_t` and to variables `stu1` and `stu2`.

   ```
   typedef struct {
         char fst_name[20],
              last_name[20];
         int  score;
         char grade;
   } student_t;
   . . .
   student_t stu1, stu2;
   ```

3. Identify the following statements as possibly valid or definitely invalid. If invalid, explain why.

   a. `student_t stulist[30];`
   b. `printf("%s", stu1);`
   c. `printf("%d %c", stu1.score, stu1.grade);`
   d. `stu2 = stu1;`
   e. `if (stu2.score == stu1.score)`
      `     printf("Equal");`
   f. `if (stu2 == stu1)`
      `        printf("Equal structures");`

g. `scan_student(&stu1);`

h. `stu2.last_name = "Martin";`

4. Write a statement that displays the initials of `stu1` (with periods).

5. How many components does variable `stu2` have?

6. Write functions `scan_student` and `print_student` for type `student_t` variables.

7. Declare an array of 40 `student_t` structures, and write a code segment that displays on separate lines the names (*last name, first name*) of all the students in the list.

8. Identify the type of each of the following references:

   a. `stu1`

   b. `stu2.score`

   c. `stu2.fst_name[3]`

   d. `stu1.grade`

9. When should you use a union type component in a structured variable?

Answers to Quick-Check Exercises

1. A structure can have components of different types, but an array's elements must all be of the same type. Use a structure for the catalog item and an array of strings for the list of student names.

2. Components of structures are accessed using the direct selection operator followed by a component name.

3. a. Valid

   b. Invalid: `printf` does not accept structured arguments.

   c. Valid

   d. Valid

   e. Valid

   f. Invalid: Equality operators cannot be used with structure types.

   g. Valid (assuming parameter type is `student_t *`)

   h. Invalid: cannot copy strings with = except in declaration (this case needs `strcpy`)

4. `printf("%c.%c.", stu1.fst_name[0],`
   `        stu1.last_name[0]);`

5. four

6. ```
   int
   scan_student(student_t *stup) /* output - student structure to
                                             fill */
   {
         int   status,
   ```
   ```

```
                char temp[4]; /* temporary storage for grade */
                status = scanf("%s%s%d%s", stu->fst_name,
                                            stu->last_name,
                                            &stu->score,
                                            temp);
                if (status == 4) {
                    status = 1;
                    (*stu).grade = temp[0];
                } else if (status != EOF) {
                    status = 0;
                }

                return (status);
            }

        void
        print_student(student_t stu) /* input - student structure to
                                              display */
        {
                printf("Student: %s, %s\n", stu.last_name,
                    stu.fst_name);
                printf("    Score: %d       Grade: %c\n", stu.score,
                    stu.grade);
        }
```

7. `student_t students[40];`

```
    for  (i = 0;  i < 40;  ++i)
        printf("%s, %s\n", students[i].last_name,
                students[i].fst_name);
```

8. a. `student_t`
    b. `int`
    c. `char`
    d. `char`

9. Use a union type component in a structured variable when the needed structure components vary depending on the value of one component.

Review Questions

1. Define a structure type called `subscriber_t` that contains the components `name`, `street_address`, and `monthly_bill` (i.e., how much the subscriber owes).

2. Write a C program that scans data to fill the variable `competition` declared below and then displays the contents of the structure with suitable labels.

```
#define STR_LENGTH 20

typedef struct {
    char event[STR_LENGTH],
         entrant[STR_LENGTH],
         country[STR_LENGTH];
    int  place;
} olympic_t;
. . .
olympic_t competition;
```

3. How would you call a function `scan_olympic` passing `competition` as an output argument?

4. Identify and correct the errors in the following program:

```
typedef struct
    char    name[15],
            start_date[15],
    double hrs_worked,
summer_help_t;

/* prototype for function scan_sum_hlp goes here */

int
main(void)
{
    struct operator;

    scan_sum_hlp(operator);
    printf("Name: %s\nStarting date: %s\nHours worked:
            %.2f\n", operator);

    return(0);
}
```

5. Define a data structure to store the following student data: gpa, major, address (consisting of street address, city, state, zip), and class schedule (consisting of up to six class records, each of which has description, time, and days components). Define whatever data types are needed.

142

Programming Projects

1. Define a structure type `auto_t` to represent an automobile. Include components for the make and model (strings), the odometer reading, the manufacture and purchase dates (use another user-defined type called `date_t`), and the gas tank (use a user-defined type `tank_t` with components for tank capacity and current fuel level, giving both in gallons). Write I/O functions `scan_date`, `scan_tank`, `scan_auto`, `print_date`, `print_tank`, and `print_auto`, and also write a driver function that repeatedly fills and displays an auto structure variable until EOF is encountered in the input file. Here is a small data set to try:

```
Mercury Sable    99842 1 18 2001 5 30 1991 16    12.5
Mazda   Navajo  123961 2 20 1993 6 15 1993 19.3 16.7
```

2. Define a structure type `element_t` to represent one element from the periodic table of elements. Components should include the atomic number (an integer); the name, chemical symbol, and class (strings); a numeric field for the atomic weight; and a seven-element array of integers for the number of electrons in each shell. The following are the components of an `element_t` structure for sodium.

```
11   Sodium  Na  alkali_metal  22.9898  2 8 1 0 0 0 0
```

Define and test I/O functions `scan_element` and `print_element`.

3. A number expressed in scientific notation is represented by its mantissa (a fraction) and its exponent (an integer). Define a type `sci_not_t` that has separate components for these two parts. Define a function `scan_sci` that takes from the input source a string representing a positive number in scientific notation, and breaks it into components for storage in a `sci_not_t` structure. The mantissa of an input value (m) should satisfy this condition: `0.1 <= m < 1.0`. Also write functions to compute the sum, difference, product, and quotient of two `sci_not_t` values. All these functions should have a result type of `sci_not_t` and should ensure that the result's mantissa is in the prescribed range. Define a `print_sci` function as well. Then, create a driver program to test your functions. Your output should be of this form:

```
Values input:  0.25000e3  0.20000e1
Sum:   0.25200e3
Difference:  0.24800e3
Product:  0.50000e3
Quotient:  0.12500e3
```

4. Microbiologists estimating the number of bacteria in a sample that contains bacteria that do not grow well on solid media may use a statistical technique called the most probable number (MPN) method. Each of five tubes of nutrient medium receives 10 ml of the sample. A second set of five tubes receives 1 ml of sample per tube, and in each of a third set of five tubes, only 0.1 ml of sample is placed. Each tube in which bacterial growth is observed is recorded as a positive, and the numbers for the three groups are combined to create a triplet such as 5-2-1, which means that all five tubes receiving 10 ml of sample show bacterial growth, only two tubes in the 1-ml group show growth, and only one of the 0.1-ml group is positive. A microbiologist would use this combination-of-positives triplet as an index to a table like the table

Table of Bacterial Concentrations for Most Probable Number Method

Combination of Positives	MPN Index/100 ml	95% Confidence Limits	
		Lower	Upper
4-2-0	22	9	56
4-2-1	26	12	65
4-3-0	27	12	67
4-3-1	33	15	77
4-4-0	34	16	80
5-0-0	23	9	86
5-0-1	30	10	110
5-0-2	40	20	140
5-1-0	30	10	120
5-1-1	50	20	150
5-1-2	60	30	180
5-2-0	50	20	170
5-2-1	70	30	210
5-2-2	90	40	250
5-3-0	80	30	250
5-3-1	110	40	300
5-3-2	140	60	360

[1]*Microbiology, An Introduction,* 7th ed. edited by Gerard J. Tortora, Berdell R. Funke, and Christine L. Case (San Francisco, California: Benjamin Cummings, 2001), p. 177.

below to determine that the most probable number of bacteria per 100 ml of the sample is 70, and 95% of the samples yielding this triplet contain between 30 and 210 bacteria per 100 ml.

Define a structure type to represent one row of the MPN table. The structure will include one string component for the combination-of-positives triplet and three integer components in which to store the associated most probable number and the lower and upper bounds of the 95% confidence range. Write a program to implement the following algorithm for generating explanations of combination-of-positives triplets.

a. Load the MPN table from a file into an array of structures called `mpn_table`.

b. Repeatedly get from the user a combination-of-positives triplet, search for it in the combination-of-positives components of `mpn_table`, and then generate a message such as:

```
For 5-2-1, MPN = 70; 95% of samples contain between 30 and
210 bacteria/ml.
```

c. Define and call the following functions.

   `load_Mpn_Table`—Takes as parameters the name of the input file, the `mpn_table` array and its maximum size. Function opens the file, fills the `mpn_table` array, and closes the file. Then it returns the actual array size as the function result. If the file contains too much data, the function should store as much data as will fit, display an error message indicating that some data has been ignored, and return the array's maximum size as its actual size.

   `search`—Takes as parameters the `mpn_table` array, its actual size, and a target string representing a combination-of-positives triplet. Returns the subscript of the structure whose combination-of-positives component matches the target or -1 if not found.

5. Numeric addresses for computers on the international network Internet are composed of four parts, separated by periods, of the form

```
xx.yy.zz.mm
```

where `xx`, `yy`, `zz`, and `mm` are positive integers. Locally, computers are usually known by a nickname as well. You are designing a program to process a list of Internet addresses, identifying all pairs of computers from the same locality. Create a structure type called `address_t` with components for the four integers of an Internet address and a fifth component in which to store an associated nickname of 10 characters. Your program should read a list of up to 100 addresses and nicknames terminated by a sentinel address of all zeros and a sentinel nickname.

Sample Data

```
111.22.3.44        platte
555.66.7.88        wabash
111.22.5.66        green
0.0.0.0            none
```

The program should display a list of messages identifying each pair of computers from the same locality—that is, each pair of computers with matching values in the first two components of the address. In the messages, the computers should be identified by their nicknames.

Example Message

```
Machines platte and green are on the same local network.
```

Follow the messages by a display of the full list of addresses and nicknames. Include in your program a `scan_address` function, a `print_address` function, and a `local_address` function. Function `local_address` should take two address structures as input parameters and return 1 (for true) if the addresses are on the same local network, and 0 (for false) otherwise.

6. The results of a survey of the households in your township have been made available. Each record contains data for one household, including a four-digit integer identification number, the annual income for the household, and the number of members of the household. You may assume that no more than 25 households were surveyed. Write a program to store the survey results into an array of user-defined structures of type `household_t`. Then perform the following analyses:

a. Print a three-column table displaying the data.
b. Calculate the average household income, and list the identification number and income of each household whose income exceeds the average.
c. Determine the percentage of households having incomes below the poverty level. The poverty level income may be computed using the formula

$$P = \$7500.00 + \$950.00 \times (m - 2)$$

where m is the number of members of each household. This formula shows that the poverty level depends on the number of family members m and the poverty level increases as m gets larger.

The following is one data set to use in testing your program.

Identification Number	Annual Income	Household Members
1041	$12,180	4
1062	13,240	3
1327	19,800	2
1483	24,458	8
1900	17,000	2
2112	19,125	7
2345	17,623	2
3210	5,200	6
3600	9,500	5
3601	11,970	2
4725	9,800	3
6217	10,000	2
9280	8,200	1

7. Design and implement a structure type to model an ideal transformer. If you have a single iron core with wire 1 coiled around the core N_1 times and wire 2 wound around the core N_2 times, and if wire 1 is attached to a source of alternating current, then the voltage in wire 1 (the input voltage V_1) is related to the voltage in wire 2 (the output voltage V_2) as

$$\frac{V_1}{V_2} = \frac{N_1}{N_2}$$

and the relationship between the input current I_1 and the output current I_2 is

$$\frac{I_1}{I_2} = \frac{N_1}{N_2}$$

A variable of type `transformer_t` should store N_1, N_2, V_1, and I_1. Also define functions `v_out` and `i_out` to compute the output voltage and current of a transformer. In addition, define functions that set each of the transformer's components to produce a desired output voltage or current. For example, function `set_n1_for_v2` should take a desired output voltage as an input parameter and a transformer as an input/output parameter and should change the component representing N_1 to produce the desired current. Also define `set_v1_for_v2`, `set_n2_for_v2`, and `set_n2_for_i2`. Include `scan_transformer` and `print_transformer` functions to facilitate I/O.

8. At a grocery store, certain categories of products sold have been established, and this information is to be computerized. Write a function to scan and store information in a structure variable whose data type is one you define—a type that includes a component that has multiple interpretations. Also write an output function and a driver function to use in testing.

    The data for each item consists of the item name (a string of less than 20 characters with no blanks), the unit cost in cents (an integer), and a character indicating the product category (`'M'` for meat, `'P'` for produce, `'D'` for dairy, `'C'` for canned goods, and `'N'` for nonfoods). The following additional data will depend on the product category.

Product Category	Additional Data
Meats	character indicating meat type (`'R'` for red meat, `'P'` for poultry, `'F'` for fish) date of packaging expiration date
Produce	character `'F'` for fruit or `'V'` for vegetable date received
Dairy	expiration date
Canned goods	expiration date (month and year only) aisle number (an integer) aisle side (letter `'A'` or `'B'`)
Nonfoods	character indicating category (`'C'` for cleaning product, `'P'` for pharmacy, `'O'` for other) aisle number (an integer) aisle side (letter `'A'` or `'B'`)

A data line for canned corn would be

```
corn   89C   11 2000   12B
```

The corn costs 89 cents, expires in November of 2000, and is displayed in aisle 12B.

9. Create a structure type to represent a battery. A `battery_t` variable's components will include the voltage, how much energy the battery is capable of storing, and how much energy it is currently storing (in joules). Define functions for input and output of batteries. Create a function called `power_device` that (a) takes the current of an electrical device (amps) and the time the device is to be powered by the battery (seconds) as input parameters and (b) takes a battery as an input/output parameter. The function first determines whether the battery's energy reserve is adequate to power the device for the prescribed time. If so, the function updates the battery's energy reserve by subtracting the energy consumed and then returns the value true (1). Otherwise it returns the value false (0) and leaves the energy reserve unchanged. Also define a function named `max_time` that takes a battery and the current of an electrical device as input parameters and returns the number of seconds the battery can operate the device before it is fully discharged. This function does not change any of the battery's component values. Write a function `recharge` that sets to the maximum capacity the battery's component representing present energy reserve. Use the following equations in your design:

$$p = vi \qquad w = pt$$

p = power in watts (W)
v = voltage in volts (V)
i = current in amps (A)
w = energy in joules (J)
t = time in seconds (s)

For this simulation, neglect any loss of energy in the transfer from battery to device.

Create a main function that declares and initializes a variable to model a 12-V automobile battery with a maximum energy storage of 5×10^6J. Use the battery to power a 4-A light for 15 minutes, and then find out how long the battery's remaining energy could power an 8-A device. After recharging the battery, recalculate how long it could operate an 8-A device.

10. In the Self-Check Exercises of Sections 11.1 and 11.2, you defined a data type `location_t` to represent a geographic location and some functions to process certain components of the type. Write functions `print_location`, `location_equal`, and `scan_location` for processing type `location_t` data, and develop a driver to use in testing this group of functions.